COLLINS
COLOUR
COOKERY

Whether cooking for an elaborate dinner party or a simple family supper, *Collins Colour Cookery* will help you with ideas and recipes for meals to remember.

Each recipe has its own full-colour photograph, to help you choose and present a dish.

Traditional favourites and exciting international dishes appear in each chapter. The recipes range from soups and starters, to meat, poultry and fish dishes, to salads, puddings and desserts – with a complete chapter on cakes and baking.

Handy 'Cook's Tips' are to be found throughout the book. These are a careful selection of helpful hints and alternative ideas, all contributed by highly experienced cookery writers.

So versatile, this is a cookery book to fit the family's needs, whatever their tastes, ages, numbers – and your budget.

With over 200 colourful recipes to choose from, there's something here for every cook.

COLLINS
COLOUR
COOKERY

First published in 1982 by
William Collins Sons & Co. Ltd.

London · Glasgow · Sydney · Auckland
Toronto · Johannesburg

Reprinted in 1983 and 1985
10 9 8 7 6 5 4 3 2 1

© 1982 William Collins Sons & Co. Ltd.

Contributors:
Barbara Croxford
Susan Graham
Audrey Hundy
Phyllis Powell
Rosemary Speller
Janet Warren
Carol Wright

All recipe photographs by Rex Bamber
Cover photographs by Rex Bamber except where indicated:
TOP ROW, left to right, reading from back to front of cover:
Cherry cake; Riviera casserole; Hague's bluff; Lancashire
hot pot; Mince pies (courtesy of Jif Lemon Bureau); Curried
chicken salad; Meringues (courtesy of Gale's Honey
Bureau); French beef (courtesy of Colman's Mustard
Kitchen); Poulet basque.
BOTTOM ROW, left to right, reading from back to front of cover:
Cream horns; Scones (courtesy of Gale's Honey Bureau);
Casserole of pheasant; Savoury cheese buns; Country
omelette; Bacon parcels with mushrooms and tomatoes;
Salad niçoise (courtesy of Colman's Mustard Kitchen);
Cream of corn soup (courtesy of Jif Lemon Bureau);
Raised pork pie.

Cover designed by Pedro Prá-Lopez

Composition in Century by Filmtype Services Ltd.,
Scarborough, North Yorkshire

Printed and bound by Graficromo s.a., Cordoba, Spain

ISBN 0 00 411227 X

Contents

Introduction | Basic recipes

A book with a colour photograph for every recipe is indeed a luxury. If you are a beginner, these illustrations help you to turn out a dish that looks as good as it tastes. If you are more experienced, you will find plenty of old favourites with a different twist, and new ideas, too. Each chapter contains dishes for every day and dishes for special occasions and entertaining.

Be sure to read the Cook's Tips below the recipes. They refer to the recipe directly above and are there to give help with that dish. Some suggest alternative serving methods and others are general hints. Knowing why a recipe method should be followed will often prevent mistakes and make cooking more relaxed and pleasurable.

Metric weights have been given with the recipes as many people now have scales with both metric and imperial measurements. Always use one method of measurement throughout and do not mix metric with imperial or your results may not be satisfactory.

Every busy cook has her favourite aids and gadgets in the kitchen and to get full use of them, careful planning is important. Planning menus for every day can be trying at times, so these colourful pages should give you some ideas.

If you have a freezer, you will be familiar with the idea of making two and freezing one. There are plenty of suitable recipes, especially for casseroles.

We are all concerned about saving fuel, and pressure cookers which cook extra quickly or slow crock pots can all be utilized to the full with this book. Microwave cooking is new to many people but is something for the future to be considered with your own special needs in mind.

From the chapter titles you will see there are recipes for all occasions and some that will double to meet different needs. The requirements of every family change with the ages of its members: children and elderly people need light, nourishing meals, while growing youngsters need something filling as well. Many families lead busy lives during the week, some have hot lunches while others have their main meal in the evening. If you can really only get together round the table at the weekend, you will want to make something special to serve and you should find plenty to interest you here.

Try planning menus one week ahead with the help of this book and you will see its wide range. Everyone who has to cook should enjoy it and – with the help of this book – we hope you will, too.

FRENCH DRESSING

4 tablespoons olive oil
$\frac{1}{2}$ level teaspoon salt
$\frac{1}{4}$ level teaspoon caster sugar
$\frac{1}{2}$ level teaspoon freshly ground pepper
2 tablespoons white wine vinegar

1. Put oil into a basin and add salt, sugar and pepper.
2. Whisk in the vinegar drop by drop and continue beating until mixture thickens slightly.

Variations
Add a few chopped fresh herbs, a little crushed garlic or a dash of mustard etc.

ASPIC JELLY
Makes 300ml or $\frac{1}{2}$ pint

15g ($\frac{1}{2}$oz) gelatine
300ml ($\frac{1}{2}$ pint) boiling water
6g ($\frac{1}{4}$oz) caster sugar
$\frac{1}{2}$ level teaspoon salt
2 tablespoons tarragon vinegar
2 tablespoons lemon juice

1. Dissolve gelatine in boiling water. Add all other ingredients.
2. Leave to cool and thicken.
3. Use as required either before or after it has set as the recipe demands.

Note
Alternatively, thicken a can of consommé with approximately 2 teaspoons gelatine. Or dilute clear meat extract or a bouillon cube with 300ml ($\frac{1}{2}$ pint) water and add approximately 2 teaspoons gelatine.

MAYONNAISE
Makes 400ml or $\frac{3}{4}$ pint

3 egg yolks
3 level teaspoons French mustard
good pinch of caster sugar
salt and pepper
400ml ($\frac{3}{4}$ pint) oil
about 2 tablespoons distilled white vinegar

1. Put the egg yolks, into a bowl with the mustard, sugar, salt and pepper.
2. Measure the oil into a jug, then add a drop at a time to the yolks, beating all the time with a wooden spoon.

3. When the mayonnaise starts to thicken the oil can be added a little more quickly.
4. When it is really thick, add a little vinegar to thin it to the right consistency.
5. Check the mayonnaise for seasoning then store it in a screw-topped jar in a cool place until it is required.
6. To make the mayonnaise in a liquidizer, put the *whole* eggs into the goblet with the mustard, sugar, salt and pepper.
7. Blend the ingredients together for a few seconds then add the oil in a steady thin stream.
8. As it starts to thicken add the oil more quickly then adjust the consistency with the vinegar.

WHITE SAUCE
Makes 300ml or $\frac{1}{2}$ pint

15g ($\frac{1}{2}$oz) butter or margarine
15g ($\frac{1}{2}$oz) flour
300ml ($\frac{1}{2}$ pint) cold milk (or milk and stock or water mixed)
salt and pepper

1. Melt the butter or margarine in a pan over a gentle heat.
2. Stir in flour and cook without browning for 2 minutes, stirring all the time.
3. Remove pan from heat and gradually beat in the liquid. Alternatively, add all the liquid and whisk thoroughly.
4. Return to heat and bring to boil, stirring well. Simmer gently for 2–3 minutes and add seasoning. If sauce is to be kept, cover it with greaseproof paper or foil to prevent a skin forming.

THICK WHITE SAUCE
Makes 300ml or $\frac{1}{2}$ pint

Make exactly as for white sauce, above, but double the quantities of butter or margarine and flour used.

CHEESE SAUCE
Makes 250ml or $\frac{1}{2}$ pint

Make up 250ml ($\frac{1}{2}$ pint) white sauce (see this page). After sauce has come to the boil and thickened, add 50-100g (2-4oz) grated cheese and $\frac{1}{2}$ level teaspoon mustard. Stir sauce over low heat until cheese melts.

SHORTCRUST PASTRY
Makes 225g or 8oz pastry

Use for sweet and savoury dishes – pies, flans, tartlets, pasties and turnovers.

225g (8oz) plain flour
1 level teaspoon salt
50g (2oz) lard
50g (2oz) butter or margarine
cold water to mix

1. Sift flour and salt into a bowl.
2. Cut fats into flour with a knife.
3. Rub fats into flour with fingertips until mixture resembles fine breadcrumbs.
4. Add water little by little, stirring with a knife until mixture forms large lumps.
5. Bring mixture together with fingertips and knead lightly into a ball.
6. Roll out briskly on a floured board. Avoid stretching the pastry.

Note
Baking temperature: moderately hot, 200°C (400°F) or gas 6.

CHOUX PASTRY
Makes 65g (2½oz) pastry

Use for éclairs, choux buns, savoury puffs and gougère.

65g (2½oz) plain flour
pinch of salt
50g (2oz) margarine or butter
150ml (¼ pint) water
2 medium eggs, beaten

1. Sift flour and salt into a bowl.
2. Put fat into a pan with the water.
3. Heat gently until fat melts and water is boiling.
4. Take pan off heat and add the flour all in one go.
5. Beat mixture well.
6. Put pan back on a gentle heat and continue beating the mixture until it leaves the side of the pan and forms a soft mass in the centre. Cool for 2 minutes.
7. Very gradually, a teaspoon at a time, beat in the egg until you have a thick and shiny dough.
8. Use at once.

SUET CRUST PASTRY
Makes 225g or 8oz pastry

Use for sweet and savoury dishes – fruit layer puddings, meat puddings and dumplings.

225g (8oz) self-raising flour
good pinch of salt
110g (4oz) shredded suet (from a packet)
cold water to mix

1. Simply mix flour, salt and suet with enough cold water to give a fairly soft dough.
2. Knead very lightly before using.

FLAKY PASTRY
Makes 225g or 8oz pastry

Use for pies, vanilla slices, sausage rolls.

225g (8oz) plain flour
1 level teaspoon salt
75g (3oz) lard
75g (3oz) butter or margarine
1 teaspoon lemon juice
water to mix

1. Sift flour and salt into a bowl. Blend the fats on a plate and mark into four portions.
2. Rub one portion into the flour until it resembles fine breadcrumbs.
3. Mix to a smooth dough with lemon juice and water.
4. Knead dough lightly and roll it out on a floured surface into an oblong.
5. Dot two-thirds of the pastry with second portion of fat.
6. Fold the bottom third up and the top third over into an envelope shape.
7. Allow pastry to relax for 10 minutes in a cold place. This is especially important in warm weather.
8. Repeat the whole process until all the fat is used up.
9. Fold pastry in two, roll out to 5mm–1cm (¼–½ inch) thick and use as required.
Note
Baking temperature: hot, 220°C (425°F) or gas 7.

PUFF PASTRY
Makes 225g or 8oz pastry

Keep everything including hands very cold for this pastry.

225g (8oz) plain flour
½ level teaspoon salt
225g (8oz) unsalted butter in a block or 110g (4oz) cooking fat and 110g (4oz) margarine mashed and formed into a block
2 teaspoons lemon juice
6–8 tablespoons very cold water

1. Sift flour and salt into a bowl.
2. Chill the fat if soft. Rub 15g (½oz) fat into flour.
3. Mix to a dough with lemon juice and water.
4. Roll out dough to twice the length of the block of fat. Place fat on dough and fold dough down over it, sealing edges well with a rolling pin.
5. Give pastry one half turn and roll gently out into a long strip.
6. Fold dough in three, envelope style, and leave, covered, in a cold place for 30 minutes.
7. Repeat turning, rolling and folding six times.
8. Leave pastry to relax for 30 minutes between rollings and before use.
Note
Baking temperature: hot 230°C (450°F) or gas 8.

CHEESE PASTRY
Makes 225g or 8oz pastry

Use for savoury pies, canapé bases, cheese straws and savoury flans.

225g (8oz) self-raising flour
1 level teaspoon salt
pinch of cayenne pepper
50g (2oz) lard
50g (2oz) butter or margarine
150g (5oz) cheese, grated
1–2 egg yolks
cold water to mix

1. Sift flour, salt and pepper into a bowl.
2. Cut fats into flour with a knife.
3. Rub fats into flour with fingertips until mixture resembles fine breadcrumbs. Add cheese.
4. Mix in egg, then add water little by little, stirring with a knife until mixture forms large lumps.
5. Bring mixture together with fingertips and knead lightly into a ball.
6. Roll out briskly on a floured board. Avoid stretching the pastry.

Note
Baking temperature: moderate, 180°C (350°F) or gas 4.

PANCAKE BATTER
Makes 300ml or ½ pint

110g (4oz) plain flour
pinch of salt
1 egg
300ml (½ pint) cold milk
1 tablespoon oil

1. Sift flour and salt into a bowl.
2. Make a well in the centre and break egg into it.
3. Gradually beat in half the milk and continue beating until batter is smooth.
4. Fold in rest of milk with oil.

Baking blind means to bake a tart or flan empty, ready to fill with a hot or cold, cooked filling. To do this, first line the flan or pie plate with thinly rolled out pastry. Ease it gently into a flan ring or flan mould with a loose base, using your thumb. Trim edges carefully with sharp knife and do not stretch the pastry. Then prick well with a fork or place a round of greaseproof paper in the base and a heaped handful of baking beans – raw hard-baked haricot beans. (Or use hard-baked crusts.)
About 7 minutes before end of cooking, carefully remove flan ring from pastry shape and put flan back on baking sheet. At the same time remove beans or crusts and paper, to allow base of pastry to brown. Cool on a wire tray or serve hot – see individual recipes for instructions.

Useful weights and measures

The ingredients in this book are given in metric and imperial measures; follow either the metric or imperial measures in the recipes as they are not interchangeable.

When using metric measures, in some cases it has been necessary to cut down the amount of liquid used or increase the gram weight slightly. This is in order to achieve a balanced recipe and the correct consistency, because 1 ounce equals, in fact, 28.35 grams, but for convenience the recipes in this book have been converted on the basis that 1 ounce equals 25 grams.

For reference, the following tables will be helpful:

SOLID MEASURES

Grams (g)	Ounces (oz)	Pounds (lb)
25	1	
50	2	
75	3	
100	4	$\frac{1}{4}$lb
225	8	$\frac{1}{2}$lb
350	12	$\frac{3}{4}$lb
450	16	1lb
500 (0.5 kilo)		
1000 (1 kilo)		$2\frac{1}{4}$lb

LIQUID MEASURES

Millilitres (ml)	Fluid Ounces (fl oz)	Imperial Pints	Australian Metric Cup
125	4		$\frac{1}{2}$
150	5	$\frac{1}{4}$	
250	8		1
300	10	$\frac{1}{2}$	
350	12		
400	15	$\frac{3}{4}$	
600	20	1	
1000 (1 litre)	35	$1\frac{3}{4}$	

NOTES FOR AUSTRALIAN USERS

It is important to remember that the Australian tablespoon differs from the British tablespoon. The British *standard* tablespoon holds 17.7 millilitres, the British *metric* tablespoon holds 15 millilitres and the *Australian* tablespoon holds 20 millilitres. A teaspoon holds about 5 millilitres in both countries.

Here are some cup and spoon equivalents to help with ingredients and measures in the book:

CUP MEASURES
(Using the 250-ml cup)

1 cup flour	100g (4oz)
1 cup sugar	225g (8oz)
1 cup icing sugar	150g (5oz)
1 cup shortening	225g (8oz)
1 cup honey, golden syrup etc	275g (10oz)
1 cup brown sugar, lightly packed	100g (4oz)
1 cup brown sugar, tightly packed	150g (5oz)
1 cup soft breadcrumbs	50g (2oz)
1 cup dry breadcrumbs, made from fresh bread	75g (3oz)
1 cup packet dry breadcrumbs	100g (4oz)
1 cup rice, uncooked	175g (6oz)
1 cup rice, cooked	150g (5oz)
1 cup dried fruit	100g (4oz)
1 cup grated cheese	100g (4oz)
1 cup chopped nuts	100g (4oz)

SPOON MEASURES

	Level tablespoon
25g (1oz) flour	2
25g (1oz) sugar	$1\frac{1}{2}$
25g (1oz) icing sugar	2
25g (1oz) shortening	1
25g (1oz) honey	1
25g (1oz) gelatine	2
25g (1oz) cocoa	3
25g (1oz) cornflour	$2\frac{1}{2}$
25g (1oz) custard powder	$2\frac{1}{2}$

Soups, starters and salads

There is nothing quite like home-made soup, warm and nourishing on a cold day; a good start to any meal. Soups are easy to make as they can cook while you prepare the rest of the meal. The starters in this chapter include pâté, fish appetizers, and first courses made with fruit and vegetables, too. Salads are always popular, particularly with weight-watchers.

FRENCH ONION SOUP

Serves 3–4

500g (1lb) onions
25g (1oz) butter
1 scant litre (1¾ pints) stock
salt and pepper
25g (1oz) flour
**small slices French bread,
    toasted**
Parmesan cheese, grated

1. Skin and slice the onions very thinly.
2. Melt the butter in a pan and add the onions.
3. Cover with a well fitting lid and cook very slowly for about 20 minutes, stirring occasionally, or until the onions are tender but not brown.
4. Add 900ml (1½ pints) stock to the onions.
5. Season, stir and allow to heat through. Simmer for 30 minutes.
6. Blend the flour with the remaining stock and stir into the soup.
7. Reheat and cook for 10 minutes.
8. Serve in a tureen with the toasted French bread floating on top. Sprinkle with cheese.

=== **COOK'S TIP** ===

Try browning the grated cheese on the French bread under the grill and only add to the soup at serving time; this can also be good on top of other thin soups such as mixed vegetable or chicken broth, making them more substantial supper dishes.

CREAM OF CORN SOUP

Serves 4–6

2 cans (200g or 7oz) sweetcorn
600ml (1 pint) chicken stock
squeeze of lemon juice
50g (2oz) butter
50g (2oz) flour
600ml (1 pint) milk
4 tablespoons single cream
watercress to garnish

1. Empty sweetcorn into a saucepan with stock and lemon juice, and cook for 20 minutes.
2. Melt butter in a pan, add flour and cook for 2 minutes. Remove pan from heat and add milk, stirring continuously. Add the corn mixture and cook for 5 minutes.
3. Sieve the soup or mix in an electric blender.
4. If necessary, add extra milk to give a smooth, creamy consistency.
5. Stir in cream, reheat without boiling and serve, garnished with watercress.

=== **COOK'S TIP** ===

This soup tastes equally good if not sieved, the kernels of corn looking most attractive in the creamy soup. For a chowder or chunky soup, try adding a 200g (7oz) can tuna to the recipe. Drain oil from the tuna, flake with a fork and add at the same time as the cream. For something really different, add ½ teaspoon ground nutmeg with the fish.

△ *Delicious French onion soup is a meal in itself, ideal to serve on a chilly winter day.*

◁ *Delicate Cream of corn soup is equally good chilled and served cold.*

MINESTRONE

Serves 4

2 tablespoons oil
1 small onion, chopped
1 carrot
1 leek
1 stick celery
2 medium potatoes
75g (3oz) green peas or green
    beans
225g (8oz) cabbage
2–3 tomatoes, skinned and
    sliced
approximately 1 litre (2 pints)
    stock
25g (1oz) macaroni
25g (1oz) haricot beans, cooked
salt and pepper
grated Parmesan cheese

1. Heat oil in a large saucepan
and fry onion for a few minutes.
2. Add finely chopped carrot,
leek, celery and potatoes. Then
add peas or beans and finely
shredded cabbage, and tomatoes.
3. Stir in stock and macaroni.
Bring to the boil and simmer very
gently for 30 minutes.
4. Add haricot beans and cook for
a further 10 minutes.
5. Season with salt and pepper.
6. Pour into soup dishes and
serve sprinkled with grated
Parmesan cheese.

DUTCH PEA SOUP

Serves 6

225g (8oz) dried split peas
approximately 1.75 litres (3
    pints) water
2 pig's trotters
1 marrow bone
salt and pepper
225g (8oz) potatoes, peeled and
    sliced
3 leeks, sliced
3 sticks celery, sliced
3 onions, sliced
chopped parsley
4 frankfurter sausages

1. Wash the peas and soak them
in half the water overnight.
2. Simmer trotters and marrow
bone in remaining water for 1
hour.
3. Add the peas plus the soaking
water. Cook until soft, about 1
hour. Season well.
4. Add the potatoes, leeks, celery
and onions and cook for a further
40 minutes.
5. Remove the marrow bone and
trotters, scrape out the meat and
return this to the soup.
6. If necessary thin the soup with
a little stock. Adjust seasoning.
7. Stir in parsley and sliced
frankfurters, allow to heat and
serve.

===== COOK'S TIP =====

If pig's trotters are not available,
try using a ham bone or 3 or 4 slices
of streaky bacon, finely chopped.
Add with the soaked peas. The bone
would be removed but not the
bacon.

More or less vegetables may be △
used in Minestrone, depending on
how substantial you want the soup.

Satisfying Dutch pea soup is ▷
popular in Holland where it is
often served as a main course.

POTATO AND LEEK SOUP

Serves 6

750g (1½lb) leeks
50g (2oz) butter
225g (8oz) potatoes, peeled and chopped
1 medium onion, peeled and chopped
900ml (1½ pints) chicken stock
300ml (½ pint) milk
salt and pepper
4 tablespoons single cream
chopped chives to garnish

1. Trim the leeks removing the root and outer leaves, then slit them to the root and wash under running water. Chop into small pieces.
2. Melt the butter and cook the leeks over a low heat for 10–15 minutes, stirring occasionally.
3. Add the potatoes and onions and cook for a few minutes.
4. Add the stock, cover and simmer for about 30 minutes, until the vegetables are tender.
5. Sieve the soup (or blend in a liquidizer) then return it to the pan, add the milk and check the seasoning.
6. Bring to the boil and if liked, sieve it again to give a really smooth texture.
7. Serve with a swirl of cream in the centre and garnish with a few chopped chives.

=== COOK'S TIP ===

This recipe could be doubled to make an unusual starter for a dinner party. Add 1 teaspoon curry powder to the melted butter with the leeks to give a good flavour. This is a way to introduce the timid palate to curry flavour.

GAZPACHO 1

Serves 4

500g (1lb) tomatoes
1 small onion, sliced
1 small green pepper, sliced
1 garlic clove, crushed
1 tablespoon wine vinegar
1 tablespoon olive oil
1–2 tablespoons lemon juice
salt and pepper

Garnishes:
¼ cucumber
2 slices toast
1 red pepper
1 green pepper
3 tomatoes, skinned and de-seeded
1 Spanish onion

1. Wash the tomatoes, dry and slice roughly.
2. Put in liquidizer with the onion, pepper, garlic, vinegar and olive oil and blend together.
3. Pour into a basin, add lemon juice and seasoning to taste.
4. Chill very well in the refrigerator before serving in small soup bowls.
5. To prepare the garnishes, dice the cucumber, toast, peppers and tomatoes.
6. Finely chop the onion.
7. Put each into a bowl and hand round with the soup.

GAZPACHO 2

Serves 6

1 garlic clove
1 onion, peeled
1 pepper, de-seeded
½ cucumber
1 can (487g or 19½oz) tomato juice
6 tablespoons olive oil
4 tablespoons lemon juice
salt
cayenne pepper
2 tomatoes
2 thick slices bread, diced
25g (1oz) butter

1. In a liquidizer, blend the garlic, half the onion, half the pepper, a quarter of a cucumber and a little tomato juice (or cook for 10 minutes, then sieve them).
2. Add the remaining tomato juice, the olive oil, lemon juice, and salt and cayenne to taste. Stir well, pour into a tureen and chill.
3. Slice the remaining onion and pepper, dice the cucumber and tomatoes and place in separate bowls.
4. Fry the diced bread in the butter, turning frequently until browned. Drain and place in a serving bowl.
5. Serve the chilled soup with a slice of onion or pepper floating on the surface. The diced vegetables and croûtons are served as an accompaniment.

△ *Wholesome Potato and leek soup can also be served as a snack lunch with brown rolls or toast.*

◁ *Colourful Gazpacho is a chilled Spanish soup, ideal for summer entertaining.*

COLD RASPBERRY SOUP

Serves 4

500g (1lb) fresh raspberries
2 tablespoons honey
5 tablespoons red wine
1 small carton soured cream

1. Rub the raspberries through a fine sieve – this should give 300ml ($\frac{1}{2}$ pint) purée.
2. Put the honey, together with 2 tablespoons wine in a small saucepan and heat gently until the honey has dissolved.
3. Leave for a few minutes to cool and then stir into the raspberry purée. Stir in half the soured cream.
4. Add the rest of the wine and 200ml ($\frac{1}{3}$ pint) cold water. Stir again.
5. Chill for several hours.
6. Serve in bowls with small spoonfuls of soured cream floating on top. Serve with extra soured cream.

═══ COOK'S TIP ═══

This recipe really does need fresh raspberries as both canned and frozen raspberries have sugar or heavy syrup in with them and would make the soup too sweet. Try this when raspberries are in season and, if you like it, remember to freeze a pack or two without sugar. Label well.

You can substitute 500g (1lb) plums or damsons, but remember to remove the stones.

ONION TOP HATS

Serves 4

50g (2oz) lamb's liver
1 streaky bacon rasher
4 large onions
25g (1oz) breadcrumbs
1 dessertspoon chopped parsley
$\frac{1}{2}$ level teaspoon mixed herbs
grated rind of half a lemon
salt and pepper
50g (2oz) dripping

1. Preheat oven to moderately hot, 190°C (375°F) or gas 5.
2. Chop liver and bacon and mix together.
3. Skin the onions and put them into a pan of boiling water for 10 minutes. Drain and take out the centres.
4. Chop the centres and mix with liver and bacon, breadcrumbs, parsley, mixed herbs and lemon rind. Season well.
5. Mix thoroughly and stuff into the onions.
6. Stand the onions in a casserole dish, add the dripping and cover with foil or a lid.
7. Bake in centre of oven for 1 hour.

═══ COOK'S TIP ═══

Onions are rather neglected as a vegetable on their own, but at the beginning of winter they are cheap and these stuffed onions are very good for a starter or supper dish.

Cold raspberry soup is an unusual △ *French idea using fruit to make a cool summer soup.*

Served with baked tomatoes and ▷ *creamed potatoes, Onion top hats would make a good supper dish.*

INDIVIDUAL SALAMI AND COTTAGE CHEESE QUICHES

Serves 4

shortcrust pastry made with 150g (5oz) flour (see Basic recipes, page 7)
50g (2oz) salami, finely sliced and skinned, plus 4 slices to garnish
1 small onion, grated
½ level teaspoon mixed dried herbs
225g (8oz) cottage cheese
2 eggs, beaten
salt and pepper
few lettuce leaves and black olives to garnish

1. Preheat oven to moderately hot, 200°C (400°F) or gas 6.
2. Roll out pastry and cut to line four 10-cm (4-inch) diameter patty tins. Bring pastry well up the sides of each tin.
3. Prick base of each and line with foil and baking beans. Bake blind in centre of oven for 10 minutes.
4. Remove foil and baking beans and cook for a further 5–10 minutes, then reduce oven temperature to moderate, 180°C (350°F) or gas 4.
5. Place a few slices of salami in each flan case.
6. Blend together remaining ingredients, except for lettuce leaves and olives, and spoon over salami.
7. Bake in centre of oven for 20–25 minutes, until filling is set.
8. Garnish with lettuce leaves, black olives and extra slices of salami and serve at once.

BITTERBALLEN

Makes 28–30. Allow 2 or 3 per person

The sauce mixture may be made well in advance and kept in a refrigerator, but rolling them into small balls should be done an hour or two before serving. Ideally they should be served as soon as they have been fried and drained.

6g (¼oz) powdered gelatine
300ml (½ pint) veal stock
25g (1oz) butter
25g (1oz) flour
175g (6oz) cooked ham and veal, chopped
1 teaspoon chopped parsley
25g (1oz) Gouda cheese, grated
seasoning
75g (3oz) toasted breadcrumbs
1 small egg
fat for deep frying

1. Add gelatine to stock heating gently until thoroughly dissolved.
2. Make a white sauce using butter, flour and stock.
3. Add meat, parsley and cheese.
4. Season well, turn on to a plate and allow to cool until firm.
5. Roll into small balls, dip into breadcrumbs then into beaten egg and then into breadcrumbs again.
6. Fry in hot fat until golden brown, and drain on absorbent paper.
7. Serve in individual dishes on shredded lettuce.

=== COOK'S TIP ===

An alternative for veal would be cold cooked chicken. Remove all skin and chop finely. Large pieces will make it more difficult to get nicely shaped balls.

△ *Individual salami and cottage cheese quiches come from France, but with an Italian influence.*

◁ *Bitterballen are tasty Dutch appetizers. They should be served piping hot.*

CARIBBEAN COCKTAIL

Serves 4

2 grapefruit
100g (4oz) cooked chicken, diced
3 sticks celery, finely chopped
1 small can pineapple pieces, drained
3 tablespoons mayonnaise
salt and pepper
5 tablespoons mango chutney
4 glacé cherries

1. Halve grapefruit. Remove pulp and discard pith and pips.
2. Cut flesh into segments and combine with rest of ingredients.
3. Fill grapefruit shells, decorate each with a cherry and serve chilled.

=== COOK'S TIP ===

Use small grapefruit as this is a starter dish and meant as an appetizer. For a really special occasion, use a pair of serrated kitchen scissors to cut a zigzag edge round the top of each half grapefruit before filling.

ALGARVE BEANS

Serves 4–6

1 onion
100g (4oz) salami
100g (4oz) smoked ham or Parma ham
1 tablespoon olive oil
600ml (1 pint) chicken stock
500g (1lb) broad beans
100g (4oz) carrots
½ tablespoon tomato purée
seasoning

1. Preheat oven to cool, 140°C (275°F) or gas 1.
2. Finely chop onion, salami and smoked ham and fry in the olive oil for about 5 minutes.
3. Add chicken stock, beans, sliced carrots, tomato purée and seasoning.
4. Cover and cook in the centre of the oven for about 1 hour, until the beans and carrots are tender.
5. Serve with chunks of French bread.

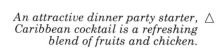

An attractive dinner party starter, △ Caribbean cocktail is a refreshing blend of fruits and chicken.

Select young broad beans when ▷ making this exciting hot first course, Algarve beans.

EDAM AND APPLE COCKTAIL

Serves 4

4 lettuce leaves, shredded
1 green apple, cored and sliced
1 red apple, cored and sliced
lemon juice
175g (6oz) Edam cheese, diced
4 tablespoons mayonnaise
1 teaspoon tomato purée
2–3 drops each Tabasco and
   Worcestershire sauce
½ teaspoon sherry (optional)

1. Place lettuce in four glass dishes. Dip apple in lemon juice and arrange with cheese on the lettuce.
2. Combine rest of ingredients together to make a sauce and either spoon it over each dish or serve it separately.

=== **COOK'S TIP** ===

Although this is a summer starter, it can be made in the winter, too. If lettuce is unavailable or expensive, look for some of the other green salad plants such as romaine lettuce, Chinese leaves or even fresh leaf spinach. Wash all salad plants well, drain and put in a covered container in the refrigerator to crispen. To use as a main course, add 100g (4oz) shelled walnuts or peanuts. This makes a light but nutritious meal.

TURKEY PANCAKES

Serves 4

175g (6oz) plain flour
pinch of salt
600ml (1 pint) milk
1 egg
15g (½oz) butter
2 level teaspoons
   curry powder
salt and pepper
350g (12oz) cooked turkey
fat for frying

1. Sieve 100g (4oz) flour and the salt into a bowl.
2. Mix with 300ml (½ pint) milk and egg to form a smooth batter. Beat well.
3. Melt the butter in a pan, add the curry powder and rest of flour. Cook slowly for about 8 minutes.
4. Add rest of milk, cook the sauce for a few minutes, then season.
5. Add the turkey, chopped in small pieces, heat through and keep hot.
6. Melt the fat in a frying pan and make the pancakes.
7. Fill with the turkey mixture and roll up.

=== **COOK'S TIP** ===

Pancakes freeze well so when making a batch double the recipe and put half in the freezer. This basic mixture can be used for sweet or savoury fillings. When cooking pancakes a good tip is to transfer the batter mixture to a jug and pour each pancake into the pan. This saves a lot of mess and allows you to tilt the heated pan when pouring in the mixture. The batter should be like thick cream and cooks in about 2 minutes on each side. Turn onto a dish. Cover well and freeze. Thaw before unrolling to fill. Either bake covered in a hot oven for 20 minutes or heat over hot water for 30 minutes.

△ *Edam and apple cocktail is a colourful summer hors d'oeuvre idea which is quick to prepare.*

◁ *Serve mouthwatering Turkey pancakes when entertaining. Chicken meat may be substituted.*

MELON COPENHAGEN

Serves 6

100g (4oz) long-grain rice
300ml (½ pint) water
½ teaspoon salt
1 melon
1 small can fruit cocktail
1 banana, peeled and sliced
12 grapes, black and green
1 orange, skinned and diced
½ lemon
Maraschino, Cognac or apricot brandy
300ml (½ pint) double cream
2½ tablespoons sugar
few drops vanilla essence
fresh fruit to decorate

1. Put rice, water and salt into a saucepan.
2. Bring to the boil and stir once. Lower heat to simmer.
3. Cover and cook for 15 minutes, or until rice is tender and liquid absorbed. Leave to cool.
4. Cut off the top of the melon and remove the seeds.
5. Hollow out the melon and cut the flesh into bite-size pieces.
6. Sprinkle with Maraschino and chill until ready to serve.
7. Drain the fruit cocktail, mix with banana, grapes, orange, melon and rice.
8. Add a little lemon juice, grated lemon rind and a touch of Maraschino. Chill until ready to serve.
9. Whip the cream, add sugar and vanilla essence.
10. Fold gently into fruit mixture. Spoon into the hollowed-out melon. Serve decorated with fresh fruit as available.

MUSHROOMS WITH CREAM

Serves 4

500g (1lb) mushrooms
50g (2oz) butter
salt and pepper
parsley
¼–½ teaspoon tarragon
chives
1 lemon
1 teaspoon tomato purée
dash Worcestershire sauce
150ml (¼ pint) single cream

1. Slice or quarter the mushrooms.
2. Heat the butter in a good-sized pan, add mushrooms and season with salt and pepper.
3. Put a few sprigs of parsley, tarragon, a few chopped chives and a sliver of lemon peel into a muslin bag and add to the pan.
4. Cover the pan and simmer until the mushrooms are tender.
5. Remove the muslin bag; blend together the tomato purée, Worcestershire sauce and cream and pour over the mushrooms.
6. Keep on a low heat until the sauce is well heated (do not allow to boil) then turn into a hot serving dish and serve with lemon wedges.

A spectacular dinner party first course, Melon Copenhagen is a luscious blend of fruits and cream. △

Mushrooms with cream and similar mushroom starters are popular in many European countries. ▷

LEMON AND CUCUMBER COCKTAIL

Serves 4

1 can (112g or 4½oz) sardines or
  other oily fish
50g (2oz) softened butter
4 lemons
6 teaspoons cucumber spread
freshly ground black pepper
1 egg white

1. Drain oil from sardines. Put them in a bowl with butter and mash together till well blended.
2. Remove top quarter of each lemon and carefully remove flesh and juice, keeping skins whole. Add flesh only to sardines and keep juice in a separate bowl.
3. Add cucumber spread to fish, then season to taste with pepper and lemon juice.
4. Whisk egg white till stiff and fold through sardine mixture.
5. Pile in lemon skins and chill.

=== **COOK'S TIP** ===

Be sure the lemons are at room temperature. Roll the lemon around on the table to soften the flesh. Cut top off and gently scoop out the flesh with a small teaspoon. Take care not to include any of the white pith in the filling as this would make it bitter. An alternative to sardines would be a small can of tuna fish. If cucumber spread is difficult to obtain, finely chop peeled cucumber and mix with a little mayonnaise.

SALAMI AND CHEESE CORNETS

Serves 4

75g (3oz) cheese, grated
1 tablespoon chutney
2 tablespoons crushed potato
  crisps
100g (4oz) sliced salami, pork
  sausage or ham sausage
a few cloves
stuffed olives and lettuce
  leaves to garnish

1. Mix together cheese, chutney and crushed crisps.
2. Make a cut from the centre to the edge of each round of meat.
3. Overlap the two cut edges to form a cornet and secure with a clove.
4. Fill with cheese mixture and top with slices of stuffed olive.
5. Serve on a bed of lettuce.

△ *Lemon shells filled with cucumber and fish, Lemon and cucumber cocktails make a refreshing meal starter.*

◁ *Choose your favourite cheese to include in these appetising Salami and cheese cornets.*

TUNA AND TOMATO PANCAKES

Serves 4

oil for frying
300ml (½ pint) pancake batter
  (see Basic recipes, page 6)
1 can tuna fish
25g (1oz) dripping
100g (4oz) mushrooms, sliced
pinch of rosemary
salt and pepper
25g (1oz) margarine
1 small onion, peeled and
  chopped
1 level tablespoon plain flour
1 can tomatoes
1 bayleaf
parsley sprig
½ level teaspoon caster sugar
few drops Worcestershire
  sauce
1 level dessertspoon tomato
  purée
1 small garlic clove, crushed
chopped parsley to garnish

1. Preheat oven to moderate,
180°C (350°F) or gas 4.
2. Make pancakes and set aside.
Allow two per person and two for
garnish.
3. Drain the oil from the fish and
flake it.
4. Melt the dripping and fry the
mushrooms for 3–4 minutes; add
them to the fish with the
rosemary and seasoning.
5. Melt the margarine in the same
pan as the mushrooms were fried
in and add the onion. Fry gently
for 2–3 minutes without
colouring. Stir in the flour and
tomatoes.
6. Stir over a gentle heat until
the mixture comes to the boil.
7. Add the bayleaf, parsley sprig,
caster sugar, Worcestershire
sauce, tomato purée, crushed
garlic, salt and pepper. Cover and
simmer for 25 minutes.
8. Sieve the sauce, then return it
to the pan and boil for a few
minutes, without the lid so it
reduces slightly.
9. Stir a little sauce into the tuna
mixture to bind the ingredients
together.
10. Divide the filling between all
but two of the pancakes, roll up
and arrange in a large ovenproof
dish.
11. Pour the remaining sauce
over the top. Cut the remaining
pancakes into strips; make each
strip about 1cm (⅓ inch) wide.
12. Lattice the top of the dish
with the strips then place in the
centre of the oven for 40–50
minutes.
13. Just before serving, sprinkle
chopped parsley in every
alternate diamond formed by the
lattice.

KIPPER CREAM

Serves 4–6

175g (6oz) kipper fillets
150ml (¼ pint) thin white sauce
  (see Basic recipes, page 6)
4 level tablespoons mayonnaise
pinch of ground nutmeg
1 egg, separated
1 dessertspoon lemon juice
salt and pepper
gelatine to set 300ml (½ pint)
3 tablespoons cold water
¼ cucumber, sliced thinly

1. Make the cream the day before
it is required. Cook the kipper
fillets and leave them to cool.
2. Remove the skin and any bones
and place the flesh in a bowl.
3. Mix in the white sauce,
mayonnaise, nutmeg, egg yolks
and lemon juice.
4. Check the mixture for
seasoning.
5. Dissolve the gelatine in the
water over a gentle heat then stir
it into the kipper mixture.
6. Finally whisk the egg whites
until stiff and, with a metal spoon,
fold into the mixture.
7. Lightly oil a 0.5 litre (1 pint) dish
and pour the cream into it.
8. Smooth over the surface then
leave to set.
9. To serve, either leave it in the
dish and arrange the cucumber
slices around the edge or loosen
the cream from the dish, turn it
on to a plate and arrange whole
cucumber slices around the base
and halved cucumber slices
around the top of the cream.

*Serve tempting Tuna and tomato △
pancakes with a cucumber and
lettuce salad.*

*Kipper cream can be served with ▷
hot toast or small savoury biscuits
for cocktail canapés.*

FISH HORNS

Makes 6

puff pastry made with 225g (8oz) flour (see Basic recipes, page 7)
milk to glaze
15g (½oz) butter
15g (½oz) flour
150ml (¼ pint) milk
salt and pepper
50g (2oz) mushrooms, chopped and cooked in butter
2 cod or similar white fish steaks, cooked and flaked
few mussels (bottled in brine, not vinegar)
cucumber and lettuce to garnish

1. Preheat oven to moderately hot, 200°C (400°F) or gas 6.
2. Roll out the pastry into a long oblong and cut it into six narrow, long strips.
3. Wind each strip round a wetted cream horn tin, just as if you were making cream horns (see page 137). Brush with milk.
4. Put on a baking sheet and bake, in centre of preheated oven, for 20 minutes.
5. Meanwhile, make the sauce. Melt the butter in a small pan; stir in the flour and cook on a low heat for 2 minutes, stirring.
6. Gradually whisk in the milk and bring to the boil, stirring, until thickened.
7. Cook gently for 2 minutes, stirring. Season with salt and pepper and mix in mushrooms, cod and mussels. Heat gently.
8. As soon as the pastry horns are cooked remove them from the tins and fill with the fish mixture. Serve at once, garnished with cucumber and lettuce, if liked.

APPLE SALADS

Serves 4

4 large eating apples
50g (2oz) cheese, finely grated
40g (1½oz) walnuts, chopped
½ head celery, chopped
150ml (¼ pint) cream, lightly whipped
juice of 1 lemon
4 walnuts

1. Wash and cut a slice off top of apples and scoop out the insides.
2. Discard cores and chop rest of apple that has been scooped out.
3. Mix with cheese, nuts and celery and fold gently into cream.
4. Pile back into the apple shells which have been sprinkled with a little lemon juice.
5. Top with a walnut and serve chilled.

=== **COOK'S TIP** ===

Choose rosy red apples and if they do not sit well on the plate cut a small slice from the base. A curved grapefruit knife would remove the centre easily. Remember to sprinkle or brush the hollowed out apples with lemon juice immediately to prevent the flesh turning brown.

△ *For an elegant dinner party first course, choose Fish horns to impress your guests.*

◁ *Apple salads are made by hollowing out eating apples and filling with a cheese and walnut mixture.*

LIVER PATE

Serves 4

350g (12oz) pig's liver
225g (8oz) fat pork
300ml ($\frac{1}{2}$ pint) milk
50g (2oz) plain flour
1 teaspoon allspice
3 tablespoons dry sherry
    (optional)
salt and pepper
50g (2oz) butter, melted

1. Preheat oven to very moderate, 170°C (325°F) or gas 3.
2. Mince liver and pork together three or four times.
3. Blend in milk, flour, allspice and sherry.
4. Stir in seasoning and butter.
5. Turn into a buttered dish and put the dish in a roasting tin of cold water.
6. Cover with foil and bake in centre of oven for about 1 hour, or until firm.
7. Leave to get quite cold and garnish with watercress.

=== COOK'S TIP ===

If you have a blender, use this to get a really smooth pâté. Chop liver and pork roughly before putting into the blender goblet with the other ingredients, liquidize until well puréed. Turn into buttered dish and cook as the recipe. Substitute chicken livers for a change of flavour. These are available fresh from your butcher or in frozen cartons at most supermarkets.

COUNTRY HERRING TERRINE

Serves 6

4 herrings or other oily fish,
    boned
salt and pepper
2 hard-boiled eggs
1 cooking apple, peeled and
    coarsely grated
50g (2oz) ground almonds
1 level teaspoon sugar
few lettuce leaves and
    cucumber slices to garnish

1. Preheat oven to moderate. 180°C (350°F) or gas 4.
2. Lightly grill herring fillets.
3. Peel off skin and pound flesh with a wooden spoon until smooth.
4. Season well with salt and pepper.
5. Slice eggs and arrange six good slices in the bottom of a greased 1 litre (approximately 1$\frac{1}{2}$ pint) ovenproof pie dish or terrine.
6. Chop the remaining egg finely and mix together with apple, ground almonds, sugar and pounded herring. Smooth into the ovenproof dish.
7. Cover with kitchen foil or lid and stand dish in a roasting tin of hot water.
8. Bake in the centre of the oven for 40 minutes.
9. Remove from the oven and leave to cool. Turn out of dish.
10. Garnish with lettuce leaves and cucumber slices and serve with fingers of toast, and butter.

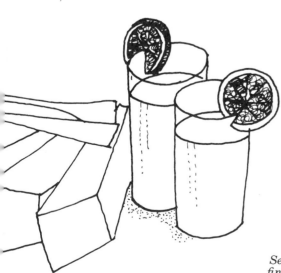

Serve popular Liver pâté with △
fingers of buttered toast and a lettuce, tomato and cucumber salad.

Country herring terrine is an ▷
attractive and unusual pâté which originated in France.

SALAD NICOISE

Serves 6

1 can (200g or 7oz) tuna fish
1 large packet frozen sliced
  beans
500g (1lb) tomatoes
½ cucumber
1 level tablespoon chopped
  fresh herbs
French dressing (see Basic
  recipes, page 6)
1 can (50g or 2oz) anchovy
  fillets
8 black olives

1. Drain the fish, flake it then place the pieces in the bottom of a shallow dish.
2. Cook the beans as directed on the packet, drain and scatter them over the fish.
3. Plunge the tomatoes into boiling water for 20 seconds. Immediately transfer them to cold water and peel off the skins.
4. Slice the tomatoes and arrange them on top of the beans.
5. Slice the cucumber thinly and arrange the slices, overlapping, on top of the tomatoes.
6. Mix the herbs with the French dressing, then sprinkle the dressing over the cucumber.
7. Lattice the top with the anchovy fillets and place a halved olive in the spaces formed by the lattice.
8. Serve chilled.

===== COOK'S TIP =====

If you are fortunate enough to grow your own herbs in the garden, or even in a pot on the window-sill, you will know the value of truly fresh herbs. A combination of two or at most three herbs is enough. When using dried herbs, remember to buy small quantities at a time so that they are constantly being replaced. Using some from a large quantity which has gone stale will not give a good flavour.

Other ingredients may be added to this salad, such as slices of hard-boiled eggs, spring onions and avocado slices.

△ *Serve colourful Salad Niçoise with brown bread and butter and lemon wedges.*

◁ *Crunchy sausage salad is an unusual blend of mushrooms, fried bread and sausages in creamy dressing.*

CRUNCH SAUSAGE SALAD

Serves 4

500g (1lb) pork sausages
25g (1oz) lard
4 slices white bread, diced
100g (4oz) mushrooms, chopped
1 garlic clove, crushed
2 tablespoons vinegar
3 tablespoons single cream
salt and pepper
1 lettuce
½ cucumber

1. Fry sausages gently in the lard, then drain and leave to cool. Slice into thick rings.
2. Fry bread, mushrooms and garlic. Drain and leave to cool.
3. Make dressing with vinegar, cream, salt and pepper.
4. Stir in the sausage rings, bread, mushrooms and garlic.
5. Chill and serve heaped in lettuce leaves, with thinly sliced cucumber.

===== COOK'S TIP =====

There are many kinds of sausage now available, including mixtures of pork and beef, and even turkey and beef, meats. Some sausages have hot seasonings and others herbs. Speciality shops have sausages from Italy, Germany and France, so try something different for this unusual way to serve sausages.

MEDITERRANEAN SALAD

Serves 4

1 packet frozen haricots verts
1 packet frozen sweetcorn
1 can pimentos, chopped
4 black olives, chopped (optional)
1 small onion, finely chopped
3 tablespoons oil
2 tablespoons vinegar
black pepper
1 teaspoon salt
2 teaspoons sugar

1. Cook the haricots verts in boiling salted water for 5 minutes.
2. Drain and run cold water over them for 1 minute.
3. Cook the sweetcorn according to the packet instructions; drain and cool.
4. Mix with pimentos, beans, olives and onion.
5. To make the dressing put the remaining ingredients into a screwtop jar and shake vigorously until thickened.
6. Blend with the vegetables and chill for several hours before serving.

═══ COOK'S TIP ═══

This salad is most attractive, making use of coloured vegetables that look well together. Small cans could be used in place of frozen vegetables but drain really well before use. Keep the ingredients for this in your store cupboard or freezer. Good in winter time too as it does not require salad plants that are often expensive at that time of year. Try also red kidney beans in place of haricot vert. They are both nutritious and colourful.

POTATO SALAD

Serves 6–8

0.75–1 kilo (1½–2lb) new potatoes
1 teaspoon finely chopped parsley
1 teaspoon finely chopped onion
1 teaspoon finely chopped chives
salt and pepper
2 tablespoons olive oil
1 tablespoon wine vinegar
cucumber slices to garnish

1. Boil the potatoes in their skins.
2. When cooked, peel the potatoes and slice while still hot.
3. Put into a salad bowl in layers, and sprinkle parsley, onion, chives and seasoning between each layer.
4. Mix the oil and vinegar and pour over the salad.
5. Garnish with cucumber slices and serve chilled.

═══ COOK'S TIP ═══

Try serving this recipe hot with cold meat. The final heating can be done just before serving. To do this chop six slices streaky bacon and fry in a large pan until crisp and golden brown. Add oil and vinegar to pan and mix well. Put in potatoes and onion and toss over low heat until warmed through. Turn into heated serving dish, sprinkle with parsley and garnish round the edge with chopped cucumber.

Colourful Mediterranean salad △ takes only minutes to prepare. Excellent served with cold meats.

In Germany Potato salad is served ▷ with hot and cold dishes. Cooked diced old potatoes may be used.

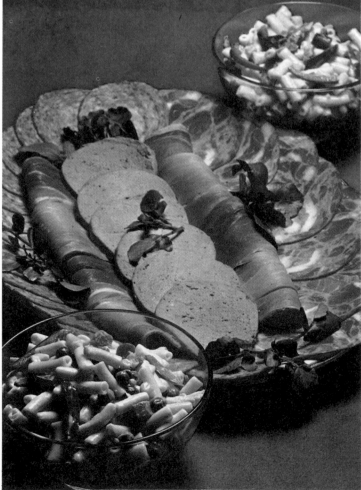

SALAD CRUNCH

Serves 4

225g (8oz) cooked potatoes
¼ small cabbage
2 red apples
juice of 1 lemon
2 tablespoons sweet and sour
   pickle
100g (4oz) Wensleydale cheese
3 tablespoons salad cream
1 tomato

1. Dice the potatoes and mix with
finely shredded cabbage in a salad
bowl.
2. Wash but do not peel the
apples and slice very thinly.
3. Dip in lemon juice and turn
into the salad bowl, reserving a
few slices for garnish.
4. Chop and add the pickle.
5. Cut the cheese into thin strips,
add to salad bowl and toss all the
ingredients gently in the salad
cream.
6. Garnish with tomato and rest
of apple slices.

=== **COOK'S TIP** ===

A salad made with cabbage and raw
vegetables should have a good,
crunchy quality only possible if the
vegetables are really fresh. Choose
white cabbage and try grating it on
the cheese side of the grater. Some
people find this texture more
palatable and also more digestible.
The ribs of the cabbage are often
quite hard and should be omitted.
Small quantities of raw turnip or
swede peeled and grated will also
add colour and flavour to this dish.
Wensleydale cheese has been
chosen for its dry, sharpish flavour
but Cheshire or Cheddar cheese
would do equally as well.

MACARONI SALAD WITH COLD MEAT

Serves 4

225g (8oz) macaroni
1 small packet frozen mixed
   vegetables
1 tomato
1 green pepper
mayonnaise
salt and pepper
lemon juice
assorted cold meats

1. Cook the macaroni in boiling,
salted water until just tender.
2. Drain and rinse through with
cold water. Leave to get quite
cold.
3. Cook the frozen vegetables,
drain and add to the macaroni.
4. Cut the tomato into strips and
de-seed it.
5. Cut the green pepper into thin
strips about 2.5cm (1 inch) long,
taking care to remove all seeds.
6. Add the tomato and pepper to
the macaroni mixture and moisten
with mayonnaise.
7. Season with salt and pepper
and a squeeze of lemon juice.
8. Arrange cold meats on a
serving dish and accompany with
small bowls of macaroni salad.

=== **COOK'S TIP** ===

There are many kinds of pasta on the
market to choose from. Shells,
corkscrews and bows are all
attractive and do not cost much
more. Just make sure you buy a size
that will fit easily on a fork. Follow
directions on the packet for cooking
times and use in recipe when cold. If
green peppers are out of season or
expensive, try a small carton of
mustard and cress tossed in with the
tomato or a bunch of watercress. Be
sure to wash this well and remove
any long or split stalks before
chopping roughly with the
tomatoes. Add to the other
ingredients.

△ *For a more substantial main
course, increase the cheese in
Salad crunch to 225g (8oz).*

◁ *Macaroni salad is also delicious
served with fish, such as canned
tuna.*

CUCUMBER AND YOGURT SALAD

Serves 4–5

1 cucumber
3 garlic cloves, chopped
2 cartons (150g or 5oz) natural yogurt (soured cream can be substituted)
2–3 tablespoons finely chopped mint
salt and freshly ground pepper

1. Slice ¼ of cucumber and set on one side to use for garnish.
2. Peel and dice remainder of cucumber.
3. Place the cucumber in a colander, sprinkle liberally with salt and set aside, under a heavy weight, for 30 minutes.
4. Mix together the garlic, yogurt, mint, salt and pepper.
5. Rinse the cucumber under cold running water.
6. Drain well and mix with the yogurt mixture.
7. Pour into serving dish and circle with slices of cucumber.
8. Serve slightly chilled as an accompaniment to lamb chops.

CRISPY BACON SALAD

Serves 4

4 streaky bacon rashers
50g (2oz) Cheddar cheese
1 stick celery
2 hard-boiled eggs
2 tomatoes
1 lettuce
1 carton soured cream or natural yogurt

1. Fry the bacon until it is crisp. Drain. Cut into small pieces.
2. Cut the cheese into tiny squares and scrub and slice the celery.
3. Quarter the hard-boiled eggs.
4. Quarter the tomatoes and wash the lettuce.
5. Turn all the ingredients into separate small bowls and serve with a bowl of soured cream or yogurt.

=== **COOK'S TIP** ===

Served in individual dishes, this is an excellent side salad. It would also make a tasty, nutritious picnic lunch or packed lunch for school children. Arrange the salad in a polythene container with tightly fitting lid. Put carton of yogurt in one corner of the same box. Spoon over the salad, just before eating.

Cooling Cucumber and yogurt salad is a popular side salad in the Eastern Mediterranean countries. △

Other salad ingredients may be added to nutritious Crispy bacon salad, such as grated carrot. ▷

CURRIED CHICKEN SALAD

Serves 4

500g (1lb) cooked chicken
50g (2oz) salted nuts
50g (2oz) sultanas
1 teaspoon curry powder
300ml (½ pint) natural yogurt
1 teaspoon chopped chives
salt

1. Cut chicken roughly. Lightly chop nuts. Mix together and add sultanas.
2. Mix curry powder, yogurt and chives together, and season with a little salt. Add this to chicken mixture.
3. Serve chicken with a lettuce and watercress salad and an egg and tomato salad.

=== **COOK'S TIP** ===

This is a good way to use up leftover roast chicken. Cut the flesh off the bone, remove all skin and cut chicken up roughly. Curry powder comes in varying strengths, some containing more hot cayenne pepper than others. Take care to taste the curry powder, yogurt and chive mixture before adding the chicken. Dishes served chilled need a stronger flavour than when served hot.

COLD CHICKEN SALAD AND CHERRIES

Serves 4–5

1 cold roasted chicken (1.5 kilo or 3lb)
500g (1lb) fresh or canned red cherries
4 tablespoons red wine
50g (2oz) lump sugar
grated rind and juice of 1 orange
1 tablespoon redcurrant jelly

1. Joint and slice the chicken; put on to a flat dish.
2. Stone all the cherries. Put wine, sugar and orange rind and juice into a pan.
3. Bring up to the boil and add the cherries.
4. Cook very slowly for about 5 minutes, until fruit is tender.
5. Stir in the redcurrant jelly. When melted, pour over the chicken.
6. Chill well and serve surrounded with lettuce leaves and accompanied with a side salad of sliced tomatoes.

=== **COOK'S TIP** ===

Green grapes and black olives are fruit that also go well with chicken. For this recipe use 225g (8oz) green grapes, washed, and 100g (4oz) black olives. The smaller olives are nice but if using the large ones, remove stones and cut in half. Cook wine, sugar and orange rind in pan and stir in redcurrant jelly. When sugar and jelly are melted, pour over chicken. Arrange grapes and olives on top of chicken.

△ *Curried chicken salad is excellent served with a white or brown rice salad.*

◁ *Luxury cold chicken salad and cherries makes an attractive summer entertaining dish.*

Meat dishes

Meat is often the heart of a meal and the most expensive item. Starters, vegetables and puddings are planned around the main dish. In this chapter there are old favourites together with new ideas from home and abroad to bring variety, which is so important when cooking meals each day. Recipes are included for summer and winter, every occasion and every budget.

SPANISH POT ROAST

Serves 4

2 tablespoons oil
1 kilo (2lb) topside, or similar
joint suitable for pot
roasting, rolled and tied
1 large onion sliced
1 green pepper, cut in rings
3 sticks celery, chopped
1 can (225g or 8oz) tomatoes
2 teaspoons tomato purée
generous pinch of brown sugar
1 dessertspoon dry mustard
200ml ($\frac{1}{3}$ pint) red wine

1. Heat oil in heavy casserole –
preferably one into which the
meat just fits.
2. Brown meat on all sides in the
hot oil.
3. Remove meat and fry onion
until soft.
4. Replace the meat, add the
pepper, celery and tomatoes.
5. Mix the tomato purée with a
little water and the brown sugar
and add to casserole.
6. Sprinkle on the mustard and
pour on the wine.
7. Cover tightly and simmer
gently for about 3 hours until
meat is tender.

===== COOK'S TIP =====

This recipe is ideally suited for
cooking in a crock pot. Pot roast
joints become tender with long,
slow cooking and this method
preserves all the flavours and
prevents shrinkage of the meat.
Consult the recipe book that came
with your pot in case it is necessary
to make adjustments to the cooking
time. It may also be necessary to
brown the joint in a pan on top of
the cooker before transferring it to
the pot. Root vegetables and
potatoes could be added to make it
a meal in one pot.

BEEF FILLET IN CRUST

Serves 4

piece beef fillet (about 1 kilo or
2lb)
butter or corn oil
strips of beef fat (optional)
salt and pepper
puff pastry made with 275g
(10oz) flour (see Basic
recipes, page 7)
1 large egg, beaten

1. Preheat oven to moderately
hot, 200°C (400°F) or gas 6.
2. Brush the meat with melted
butter or oil and, if you have
them, lay strips of fat over the
fillet. Season.
3. Put on a baking sheet.
4. Bake in centre of preheated
oven for 15 minutes per 0.5 kilo
(lb) (allow 20 minutes less on this
time if you like beef very rare).
5. Remove meat from oven, but
leave oven on.
6. Roll out the pastry to an
oblong large enough to enclose
the meat.
7. Place meat on pastry and fold
pastry over so meat is enclosed.
8. Put on a wetted baking sheet,
with the join underneath.
9. Use pastry trimmings to make
leaves or other decorative shapes
and place on top of pastry.
10. Brush all the pastry with
beaten egg.
11. Bake, in the centre of the
preheated oven, for 20 minutes, or
until golden.

===== COOK'S TIP =====

This is a recipe for a special
occasion and does require careful
timing. If you wish to serve this at
a dinner party then plan the menu
so that the other dishes can be
made early and require little
attention at serving time. Try using
frozen puff pastry. It is a good buy
and can be found in the frozen food
cabinet of most supermarkets.
Follow the directions on the
packet, it needs to be thawed before
use.

△ *Serve hearty Spanish pot roast*
with boiled potatoes, white or
brown rice or buttered noodles.

◁ *Spectacular Beef fillet in crust is a*
classic French entertaining dish.

ORANGE STEAKS

Serves 4

4 medium-sized steaks
8 small mushrooms, sliced
50g (2oz) butter
25g (1oz) blanched almonds
75g (3oz) seedless raisins
3 tablespoons white
   breadcrumbs
2 oranges
potato chips and parsley to
   garnish

1. Grill the steaks and arrange them in an ovenware dish.
2. Fry the mushrooms in half the butter and place them on top of the steaks.
3. Lightly chop the nuts and raisins together and mix with the crumbs and juice of 1 orange.
4. Place mixture on top of the mushrooms.
5. Put the dish under a hot grill for a few moments with the rest of the butter to lightly brown. Garnish with twists of sliced orange, potato chips and parsley.

FRENCH BEEF

Serves 6

50g (2oz) dripping
1 carrot, peeled and sliced
2 onions, sliced
1 kilo (2lb) topside or round of
   beef, cut into dice
50g (2oz) flour
300ml ($\frac{1}{2}$ pint) red wine
300ml ($\frac{1}{2}$ pint) beef stock
bouquet garni
$\frac{1}{2}$ teaspoon made English
   mustard
20 button mushrooms

1. Melt the dripping in a heavy pan.
2. Add carrot and onions and fry gently for a few minutes.
3. Remove, and brown the meat on all sides.
4. Remove meat and stir in the flour.
5. Add wine, stock, bouquet garni and mustard, and stir until sauce is smooth.
6. Return meat, vegetables and add button mushrooms to the pan.
7. Cover with greased paper and simmer gently for 3 hours.
8. Serve with creamed potatoes.

=== **COOK'S TIP** ===

Interesting stew recipes are always welcome, so if you have a freezer this would be a good recipe. Make double the quantity, put into two dishes, cook both and freeze one. Always be sure to mark with the date, as after three months you should use and replace with another stew.

Lamb's kidneys may be added to this stew for added flavour and richness.

Choose good quality steak when △ making Orange steaks, such as rump, porterhouse or sirloin.

Add potatoes to the ingredients of ▷ French beef to make a complete meal in one pot.

KEBABS ALFRESCO

Serves 4–8

4 lamb's kidneys
500g (1lb) thick rump steak
8 small tomatoes
100g (4oz) mushrooms
1 small can pineapple slices
1 garlic clove
salt
olive oil
pepper
12 pickled onions
2 medium cans baked beans in
   tomato sauce

1. Wash and halve the kidneys, and cut out core.
2. Cut steak into similar sized cubes.
3. Wash tomatoes and mushrooms.
4. Drain pineapple and cut into sections.
5. Crush the garlic in salt in a large dish.
6. Pour in sufficient oil to cover the base, and sprinkle with pepper.
7. Place all ingredients except pineapple on the skewers.
8. Marinate in the oil for about 15 minutes, turning the skewers occasionally.
9. Preheat the grill on the highest setting, then place kebabs under for about 4 minutes, turning them frequently.
10. Reduce the heat, thread the pineapple on the skewers and continue cooking for 4–5 minutes.
11. Meanwhile, halve the pickled onions and heat through in a saucepan with the baked beans.
12. Arrange the kebabs on top of the beans and serve immediately.

=== **COOK'S TIP** ===

To cook kebabs successfully the meat must be small enough for it to cook through at the same time as the vegetables also on the skewer, so they will not be overdone. Slices of streaky bacon rolled up or small pieces of lamb's liver would also cook well on skewers.

AUSTRIAN BEEF OLIVES

Serves 4

25g (1oz) butter
1 small onion, chopped
2 tablespoons fresh, white
   breadcrumbs
50g (2oz) mushrooms, diced
2 teaspoons freshly chopped
   parsley
pinch mixed herbs
salt and pepper
1 small egg, well beaten
4 slices rump steak about 1 kilo
   (2lb)
25g (1oz) flour, seasoned with
   salt and pepper
25g (1oz) butter
2 tablespoons oil
2 tablespoons tomato purée
300ml ($\frac{1}{2}$ pint) beef stock
1 bayleaf
2 small cartons natural yogurt
1 onion, sliced
1 tomato, sliced
$\frac{1}{2}$ cucumber, sliced
chopped chives

1. Preheat oven to moderate, 180°C (350°F) or gas 4.
2. Combine together butter, onion, breadcrumbs, mushrooms, herbs and seasoning. Bind with egg.
3. Spread over the steaks, roll up and secure with string or wooden cocktail sticks. Roll in flour.
4. Melt butter with oil in pan. Brown the meat on all sides, then gradually add tomato purée, stock and bayleaf. Cover.
5. Simmer gently for 30 minutes then transfer to a casserole and place in centre of oven for $1\frac{1}{2}$ hours.
6. Remove meat from casserole to serving dish.
7. Stir yogurt into liquor, then reheat without boiling.
8. Pour sauce over meat and serve with a salad of sliced onion, tomato and cucumber garnished with chopped chives.

△ *Transform colourful Kebabs alfresco into an entertaining dish by serving on a bed of rice.*

◁ *Remember to remove the string or cocktail sticks from Austrian beef olives before serving.*

BOEUF STROGANOFF

Serves 4–5

500g (1lb) rump steak, cut in
  2.5-cm (1-inch) strips
seasoning
generous 150ml (¼ pint) red
  wine
50g (2oz) butter or margarine
2 medium onions, sliced
100g (4oz) mushrooms, sliced
salt and black pepper
pinch of nutmeg
25g (1oz) flour
4 tablespoons tomato purée
300ml (½ pint) stock or stock
  and water
150ml (¼ pint) soured cream

1. Two hours before cooking,
sprinkle meat with seasoning and
most of the red wine, cover and
leave to stand.
2. Melt butter or margarine in a
large saucepan and fry onions and
mushrooms until soft, but not
brown.
3. Add the prepared meat and fry
gently for 4–5 minutes.
4. Stir in flour and cook for a
further 2 minutes.
5. Add tomato purée and stock,
and simmer gently for 10–15
minutes.
6. Add remaining wine and the
soured cream just before serving.
(Do not boil after cream has been
added.)

WINTER BEEF CASSEROLE

Serves 6

1 kilo (2lb) stewing steak, cut in
  5-cm (2-inch) pieces
50g (2oz) flour, seasoned with
  salt and pepper
2 tablespoons cooking oil
500g (1lb) leeks, sliced
1 small head of celery, cut in
  2.5-cm (1-inch) pieces
225g (8oz) carrots, sliced
300ml (½ pint) beer
300ml (½ pint) beef stock
225g (8oz) self-raising flour
½ level teaspoon salt
25g (1oz) butter
1½ level teaspoons dried basil
40g (1½oz) Parmesan cheese,
  grated
40g (1½oz) Cheddar cheese,
  grated
150ml (¼ pint) milk

1. Preheat oven to moderate,
180°C (350°F) or gas 4.
2. Coat steak with seasoned flour.
3. Heat oil in a frying pan, add
meat and fry until brown on all
sides.
4. Add vegetables and cook for a
further 2–3 minutes.
5. Stir in any remaining flour
from the meat. Pour in beer and
stock and bring to the boil.
6. Transfer to a 1.75 litre (3 pint)
casserole, cover and cook in
centre of oven for about 1½–2
hours until meat is tender.
7. Meanwhile mix flour and salt
together and rub in butter. Mix in
basil and half the cheese.
8. About 30 minutes before
serving casserole, increase oven
heat to moderately hot, 190°C
(375°F) or gas 5.
9. Bind flour and cheese mixture
with milk, then roll out on floured
surface to 1cm (½ inch) thick. Cut
into triangles.
10. Remove cover from casserole.
Adjust seasoning. Arrange scone
triangles on top. Sprinkle with
remaining cheese. Return to oven
and bake for about 15 minutes.
11. Serve at once with green
beans.

Boeuf Stroganoff is a classic △
*Russian dish invented by the chef
of the Stroganoff family in
Leningrad.*

Winter beef casserole freezes well. ▷
*Make and freeze the cheese scone
topping separately.*

STEAK AND KIDNEY PIE

Serves 4–6

**750g (1½lb) good quality stewing
    steak**
100g (4oz) ox kidney
**25g (1oz) flour, seasoned with
    salt and pepper**
about 300ml (½ pint) beef stock
**puff pastry made with 225g
    (8oz) flour (see Basic recipes,
    page 7)**
1 egg, beaten

1. Cut the meat into large
squares.
2. Wash and cut up the kidney
and discard any core.
3. Toss the meat and kidney in
seasoned flour.
4. Put the stock, meat and kidney
in a pan and simmer for 2 hours,
stirring occasionally.
5. When meat is nearly done,
preheat oven to moderately hot
200°C (400°F) or gas 6.
6. Put the cooked meat in an oval
pie dish with most of the stock.
Allow to cool.
7. Roll out the pastry and cut a
strip off to put on the edge of pie
dish.
8. Wet edge of dish and put pastry
strip in place. Then wet pastry
strip.
9. Use rest of pastry to make a lid
for the pie and put in place.
10. Seal pastry edges, knock up
with the blade of a knife and flute
by pinching between thumb and
forefinger.
11. Using pastry trimmings to
make leaves for the top of the pie.
Decorate as in the picture.
12. Brush all pastry with beaten
egg.
13. Make a small hole in the top
of the pie.
14. Bake, in the centre of the
preheated oven for 20 minutes
then reduce heat to moderate,
180°C (350°F) or gas 4 and cook
for 15 minutes more or until
golden brown.

═══ COOK'S TIP ═══

For a very special pie, 100g (4oz)
sliced mushrooms could be added to
the meat when put to cool before
being topped with pastry. If you are
in a hurry, frozen puff pastry makes
an excellent pie crust.

SPEEDY GOULASH

Serves 4

1 medium can stewing steak
1 medium can tomatoes
**1 small can red peppers,
    chopped**
1 teaspoon paprika
1 small can mushrooms
**150g (5oz) boiled long-grain rice
    (raw weight)**
1 small carton natural yogurt

1. Heat the stewing steak with
tomatoes and red peppers.
2. Stir in paprika pepper and
bring to the boil.
3. Serve in a hot dish
accompanied by boiled rice with
mushrooms and yogurt.

═══ COOK'S TIP ═══

Boiled noodles make a change from
rice and cook in half the time.
Corned beef, cubed, could replace
stewing steak.

Speedy goulash makes use of
cans and dry stores, this cuts
preparation time and is also useful
if friends drop in unexpectedly.
Care in planning and shopping for
menus should always include a
thought for the store cupboard.
Have three or four recipes of this
type for main courses and puddings
and keep the ingredients at hand.
Always remember to replace these
ingredients as they are used.

△ *Traditional Steak and kidney pie
is an ever-popular dish,
sumptuously served here on a
silver platter.*

◁ *Speedy goulash is made with
canned stewing steak served with
mushrooms mixed with rice.*

BOEUF ROUSSY

Serves 4–6

750g (1½lb) stewing steak
6 tablespoons oil
25g (1oz) butter
3–4 shallots or very small
    onions
1 kilo (2lb) carrots, peeled and
    cut into strips lengthways
salt and pepper
pinch of nutmeg

1. Preheat oven to very moderate,
170°C (325°F) or gas 3.
2. Trim meat and cut into
individual portions.
3. Heat oil and butter together in
a flameproof casserole and fry
shallots or onions until lightly
browned.
4. Add meat and brown on all
sides.
5. Add carrots and season well
with salt, pepper and nutmeg.
6. Cover closely with lid or foil
and cook in centre of oven for 2
hours, or until meat is tender.
7. Serve with creamed potatoes
and a green vegetable.

Slow Cooker Method
1. Proceed as stages 2–5 above,
inclusive, but using a saucepan.
2. Transfer to a preheated slow
cooker. Cook on High for 30
minutes and on Low for 6–8
hours.

STEAK COBBLER

Serves 4

1 large can stewed steak
1 large packet frozen, mixed
    vegetables, thawed
1 packet scone mix
100g (4oz) cheese, grated

1. Preheat oven to moderately
hot, 190°C (375°F) or gas 5.
2. Mix steak and vegetables in an
ovenware dish.
2. Make up scone mix as directed
on packet and add cheese.
3. Pat out flat and cut into 10
rounds with a pastry cutter.
4. Arrange on top of dish and
cook on second shelf down of oven
for 30 minutes.

=== **COOK'S TIP** ===

This is another quick recipe using
convenience foods. Time could be
saved by cooking the frozen
vegetables in a small quantity of
water before adding to the steak.
The cobbler or topping can be
varied by omitting the cheese and
using one teaspoon dried mixed
herbs or two level teaspoons curry
powder. Using a pastry cutter gives
individual servings but the scone
could cover the steak as a normal
pie crust. Remember to cut a small
hole in the top for steam to escape.

*Boeuf Roussy is a French country △
casserole, sweet in flavour because
of the high proportion of carrots.*

*Steak cobbler is a quick to make, ▷
nourishing dish made with frozen
mixed vegetables and packet
scone mix.*

MEAT LOAF IN PASTRY

Serves 6

shortcrust pastry made with
   275g (10oz) flour (see Basic
   recipes, page 7)
½ can (280g or 10½oz) condensed
   mushroom soup (undiluted)
5 tablespoons tomato ketchup
1 medium egg, beaten
1 small onion, skinned and
   chopped
salt and pepper
25g (1oz) flour
4 heaped tablespoons fresh
   white breadcrumbs
750g (1½lb) raw minced beef
cucumber and spring onions to
   garnish

1. Preheat oven to moderately
hot, 190°C (375°F) or gas 5.
2. Roll out the pastry; cut off a
third, use rest to line a 0.5 kilo
(1lb) loaf tin.
3. Mix the rest of the ingredients
together (reserve a little egg to
glaze) and put into pastry-lined
tin.
4. Wet edges of pastry in tin with
a little egg.
5. Use reserved pastry to make a
lid and put in position.
6. Press pastry edges well to seal.
Brush with egg.
7. Bake loaf, in centre of the
preheated oven, for 1½ hours,
covering pastry with foil after the
first 40 minutes.
8. Leave to cool in the tin.
9. Turn out to serve when cold.
10. Garnish with cucumber and
spring onions if liked.

=== COOK'S TIP ===

Condensed soup is a good base for
a ready-made sauce. Cream of
mushroom, asparagus and celery
can all be used this way. Dilute
with ½ quantity of liquid called for
in soup using milk. These make
excellent pouring sauces to be
handed round separately. A
tablespoon of cooking sherry added
at the last minute makes the sauce
something special.

MUSHROOM BEEFBURGERS

Serves 4

1 onion
500g (1lb) minced beef
salt and pepper
1 can condensed mushroom
   soup
175g (6oz) fresh breadcrumbs
fat for frying
2 tomatoes, quartered

1. Chop onion quite finely and
mix with minced beef, seasoning,
soup and enough breadcrumbs for
the mixture to be not too wet.
2. Divide the mixture into eight
small beefburger shapes and coat
with remaining breadcrumbs.
3. Fry gently in hot fat for about
15 minutes on each side.
4. Garnish with tomato quarters
and watercress and serve with
baked beans.

CHILLI CON CARNE

Serves 4–6

175g (6oz) red kidney beans
1 tablespoon corn oil
750g (1½lb) minced beef
2 medium onions, peeled and
   chopped
1 garlic clove, peeled and
   crushed
1 can (425g or 15oz) peeled
   tomatoes
1 level dessertspoon mild chilli
   powder
good pinch of sugar
1 tablespoon vinegar
dash of Tabasco sauce
salt and pepper

1. Soak beans overnight in cold
water to cover. Boil rapidly for at
least 10 minutes.
2. Preheat oven to very moderate,
170°C (325°F) or gas 3.
3. Heat oil in a heavy saucepan
and fry the minced beef until
lightly browned. Add onions and
garlic and continue cooking
gently for a further 5 minutes.
4. Stir in drained beans, tomatoes
with their juice, chilli powder and
sugar blended with vinegar. Add
Tabasco sauce and season to taste
with salt and pepper. Transfer to
a casserole.
5. Cover closely with lid or foil
and cook in centre of oven for
about 2 hours, or until meat is
tender.
6. Serve with boiled rice.

△ *Meat loaf in pastry makes an
excellent summertime main course.
Ideal to take on picnics.*

◁ *Popular with children, serve
Mushroom beefburgers in rolls or
buns and accompany with pickles.*

MEATBALL CURRY

Serves 4

40g (1½oz) margarine
350g (12oz) onions, peeled and
    sliced
2 level teaspoons turmeric
¼ level teaspoon ground ginger
¼ level teaspoon ground
    cinnamon
2 level teaspoons curry powder
½ level teaspoon curry paste
large pinch cayenne pepper
1 level teaspoon salt
1 bay leaf
1 small can tomatoes
400ml (¾ pint) stock
2 tablespoons coconut milk
    (to make this, infuse 2 level
    teaspoons desiccated
    coconut in 2 tablespoons
    boiling water for 30 minutes
    and then strain the mixture)
500g (1lb) raw minced beef
50g (2oz) fresh breadcrumbs
½ level teaspoon dried mixed
    herbs
1 large egg
salt and pepper
15g (½oz) plain flour, seasoned
    with salt and pepper
15g (½oz) lard
1 small dessert apple
¼ small cauliflower

1. Make the sauce the day before
it is required.
2. Melt the margarine in a large
pan and fry the onions until they
start to soften.
3. Stir in the turmeric, ground
ginger, ground cinnamon, curry
powder and paste, chilli powder,
salt and bay leaves.
4. Allow these ingredients to fry
for about 10 minutes.
5. Pour in the can of tomatoes
with the stock and coconut liquid
and stir the curry sauce until it
comes to the boil.
6. Reduce the heat, cover the pan
and simmer the sauce for about 1
hour.
7. When the sauce has cooked
transfer it to a bowl and leave it
in a cool place for the next day.
8. Mix the minced beef with the
breadcrumbs and herbs.
9. Beat the egg and work it into
the meat with the seasoning.
10. Divide the mixture into 12
pieces and roll each into a ball.
11. Toss them in the seasoned
flour so they are well coated.
12. Melt the lard in a frying pan
and fry the balls until they are
evenly brown.
13. Transfer them to the curry
sauce and cook gently for about 1
hour.
14. Peel, quarter, core and dice
the apple and cut the cauliflower
into small sprigs.
15. Add the apple and the
cauliflower to the curry 20
minutes before the end of the
cooking time.
16. Serve the curry in a large
dish.

ACCOMPANIMENTS

Curry is usually served with plain
boiled rice (long grain) and a
selection of the following served
in individual dishes:
1. Salted almonds.
2. Mango chutney.
3. Coconut – if fresh, scoop flesh
out of the shell and cut off dark
outer skin. Grate on coarse
grater. Desiccated coconut is an
alternative.
4. Sliced bananas sprinkled with
lemon juice. Much better than
water to remove the fiery feel in
the mouth.
5. Tomato and onion. Slices of
peeled tomato topped with grated
onion.
6. Hard-boiled eggs. Cut in half,
put yolks and white in separate
bowls and chop whites. Put white
round outside and pile sieved
yolks in centre of dish.
7. Cucumber and yogurt. Dice ½
cucumber including skin and add
to a carton of natural yogurt.
8. Dahl, a purée of lentils highly
seasoned with curry powder.

*A hot and spicy Mexican △
speciality, serve Chilli con carne
when casually entertaining
friends.*

*With the bowls of accompaniments, ▷
Meatball curry makes a colourful
spread for all occasions.*

NOODLES WITH MEAT SAUCE

Serves 4

1 onion, peeled
50g (2oz) mushrooms, peeled
225g (8oz) minced meat
40g (1½oz) butter
300ml (½ pint) stock
salt and pepper
350g (12oz) noodles
grated Parmesan cheese
3 tablespoons red wine
1 tablespoon chopped parsley
2 tablespoons single cream, top
  of the milk or natural yogurt
3 tablespoons cooked peas

1. Chop onion and mushrooms
finely, mix with meat and fry
gently in 15g (½oz) butter for 5
minutes.
2. Add stock, then season and
simmer for 20–30 minutes, until
meat is tender.
3. Meanwhile, cook noodles in
boiling, salted water for 8–10
minutes, then drain well.
4. Toss in the rest of the butter
and some cheese.
5. Add wine, parsley, cream and
peas to meat.
6. Cook for 2–3 minutes.
7. Pile noodles on a hot dish and
pour sauce over.

=== **COOK'S TIP** ===

Adding 2 or 3 drops of vegetable oil
to the water when cooking noodles
will help prevent them sticking
together. Immediately after
draining, rinse quickly with cold
water and drain again. This is also
to prevent sticking.
  If necessary to keep noodles hot
either leave in strainer, or put in
greased dish, over hot water, cover
and keep over low heat. The meat
sauce can be added at serving time.

NEAPOLITAN LAMB CHOPS

Serves 4

4 best end neck of lamb chops
3 tablespoons chutney
1 tablespoon clear honey
½ teaspoon mixed herbs
1 tablespoon made mustard
1 beef stock cube
salt and pepper

1. Place the chops in a frying pan.
2. Mix together the chutney,
honey, herbs, mustard and the
crumbled stock cube. Season and
spoon half this mixture over the
chops.
3. Fry the chops in their own fat
for 15 minutes.
4. Turn chops over and spread
them with the remaining mixture,
cooking for a further 15 minutes.

=== **COOK'S TIP** ===

Best end of neck lamb chops are a
more economical cut of chops and,
although they are not always a tidy
shape, they are just as tasty. Be
sure to trim off any excess fat from
the chops before cooking in the
chutney mixture. To cook in the
oven use a casserole dish, cover
with a lid and cook at 180°C (350°F)
or gas 4 for 1 hour, remove lid and
cook for a further 15 minutes.

△ *Serve Noodles with meat sauce
with a tossed green salad. For a
change, pour the sauce over
spaghetti or rice.*

◁ *Delicious Neapolitan lamb chops
can be served with baked jacket
potatoes, cooked in the oven at the
same time.*

PARTY CHOPS

Serves 6

6 loin of lamb chops
salt and pepper
puff pastry made with 450g
(1lb) flour (see Basic recipes,
page 7)
1 large egg, beaten
tomato and watercress to
garnish

1. Preheat oven to moderately hot, 200°C (400°F) or gas 6.
2. Trim the excess fat off the chops.
3. Put the chops in a baking tin and season with salt and pepper.
4. Cook in centre of preheated oven for 45 minutes then drain on absorbent paper. Leave oven on.
5. Roll out the pastry and cut into six oblongs.
6. Put a chop in the centre of each oblong.
7. Brush pastry edges with egg and fold pastry over so chop is covered and its shape is apparent.
8. Put pastry-covered chops on a baking sheet with the joins underneath.
9. Use the trimmings to make leaves to decorate top of each pastry shape.
10. Brush all pastry with egg.
11. Bake, in centre of preheated oven, for 25–30 minutes or until golden brown.
12. Garnish as the picture, if liked.

COOK'S TIP

Chops cooked this way are novel and tasty but time must be planned carefully for rolling out pastry and decorating.

These chops would go down well at a picnic but it would be an idea to remove the chop bones after the initial cooking and before putting in the pastry cover.

BELGIAN CHOPS

Serves 6

225g (8oz) pork sausagemeat
6 lamb chops
2 oranges, peeled and thinly
sliced
salt
freshly ground black pepper
150ml (¼ pint) cider
watercress and fresh orange
slices to garnish

1. Preheat oven to moderate, 180°C (350°F) or gas 4.
2. Divide sausagemeat into six pieces. Fill cavity of each chop with sausagemeat and fasten with a wooden cocktail stick.
3. Brown very quickly on both sides under a hot grill.
4. Arrange orange slices in a casserole, season well and arrange chops on top. Add cider.
5. Cover closely with lid or foil and cook in centre of oven for about 1 hour, or until meat is tender, removing the lid for the last 10 minutes of cooking time.
6. Serve garnished with watercress and fresh orange slices.

COOK'S TIP

Recipes using cider are a useful addition to your menus. It is not as expensive as wine and more acceptable to children. It helps tenderize the meat as well as giving it a piquant flavour. Use in stews in place of the stock or the liquid. In this recipe, sausagemeat was suggested to stuff the chops but a thyme or lemon breadcrumb stuffing would go well with the lamb.

When time is short, use frozen puff △ pastry to make elegant Party chops.

Belgian chops are a tasty new way ▷ to serve lamb chops; accompany with boiled potatoes or rice.

BARBECUE CHOPS AND SAUSAGES

For the main course allow 1 chop and 2 sausages per person with corn cobs, a good supply of fried onions and a fresh green salad with whole tomatoes. Serve soft rolls and French bread to eat with the meat and, of course, have some barbecue sauce to lavishly coat the food while cooking.

sausages
lamb cutlets
cooking oil
onions, peeled and sliced
soft rolls

1. Thread the sausages on to a pair of long skewers so they are easier to turn. Have no more than 6 sausages per pair of skewers.
2. Brush the cutlets and the sausages with cooking oil.
3. Place them over the fire and cook them, brushing the food with barbecue sauce occasionally, until the food is brown all over and tender.
4. Fry the onions in a little oil in a pan over the fire, turning them frequently.
5. Serve the chops in serviettes and the sausages in rolls with fried onions.

BARBECUE SAUCE

Makes about 300ml (½ pint)

1 can (400g or 14oz) tomatoes
1 tablespoon tomato ketchup
1 dessertspoon vinegar
2 level tablespoons sweet chutney
1 level dessertspoon horseradish sauce
3 teaspoons Worcestershire sauce
salt and pepper

1. Sieve the tomatoes and their juice into a bowl.
2. Stir in the other ingredients to make a spicy sauce and season with salt and pepper.
3. The sauce can be made the day before it is required and stored in a covered glass bowl.

=== **COOK'S TIP** ===

This barbecue sauce could be used with pork chops or pieces of chicken equally well.

△ *In the summer, it is fun to eat out of doors: Barbecue chops and sausages are a good choice.*

◁ *Try mouthwatering Lamb cutlets Portugaise with creamed potatoes and a green vegetable, like broccoli.*

LAMB CUTLETS PORTUGAISE

Serves 4

8 lamb cutlets
2–3 tablespoons cooking oil
1 medium onion
15g (½oz) plain flour
300ml (½ pint) stock
2 teaspoons tomato purée
½ teaspoon salt
large pinch of pepper
1 teaspoon sugar
1 can (225g or 8oz) tomatoes

1. Trim excess fat from cutlets. Fry gently on both sides in 2 tablespoons oil till just brown. Remove from pan.
2. Fry peeled and chopped onion for 3–4 minutes. Add rest of oil and stir in flour. Cook till well browned.
3. Mix stock and purée with salt, pepper and sugar. Add to flour mixture, stirring until it boils and thickens.
4. Cut tomatoes in small pieces. Add to sauce and simmer.
5. Return cutlets to pan. Cover with lid and simmer for 10 minutes till cooked.
6. Serve with boiled rice.

=== **COOK'S TIP** ===

Another serving suggestion is to use brown rice as it can add a nutty flavour to the dish. Brown rice grains have had less of the outer coating polished off and are more nutritious and filling. It is obtainable in most supermarkets or health food stores and while it takes longer to cook than white rice it makes an interesting change. Add 100g (4oz) sliced mushrooms to the rice for another variation.

MINTED LAMB CUTLETS

Serves 6

6 lamb cutlets
salt and pepper
2 tablespoons corn oil
1 small onion, peeled and diced
2 sprigs mint leaves
½ level teaspoon caster sugar
300ml (½ pint) aspic jelly
2 tablespoons malt vinegar
watercress to garnish

1. Using a sharp knife trim any excess fat from the cutlets then trim the meat from the last 1cm (½ inch) of the bone. Season.
2. Heat the oil in a frying pan, add the onion and the cutlets and fry on both sides for about 5 minutes.
3. Leave them to cool.
4. Chop the mint with the sugar and stir it into the aspic jelly with the vinegar. Check seasoning.
5. Leave on one side to cool, though not set.
6. Arrange the cutlets down either side of a serving dish with the bones pointing out.
7. Spoon a little aspic jelly over each so they are coated. Leave the rest to set, then chop it roughly with a wet knife.
8. Heap the aspic down the centre of the lines of chops and place watercress sprigs at either end.
9. Place a cutlet frill on the end of each cutlet.

JELLIED LAMB SLICES

Serves 4

15g (½oz) gelatine
400ml (¾ pint) rich meat stock
juice of ½ lemon
salt and pepper
8 thin slices cold lamb
2 hard-boiled eggs
3 young cooked carrots
50g (2oz) cooked fresh peas

1. Put the gelatine into the stock.
2. Stir over a very low heat until dissolved.
3. Add the lemon juice and leave to get cold but do not allow to set.
4. Arrange the lamb in a dish and slice the eggs and the carrots and put over the meat.
5. Scatter the peas over the lamb, then pour the jelly over. Leave to set.
6. Serve with a green salad.

===== COOK'S TIP =====

Any cooked meat would look attractive served this way under jelly and garnished with cooked vegetables or salad. Try, for example, sliced turkey with asparagus spears; pork with slices of beetroot; red eating apples dipped in lemon juice, or beef with artichoke hearts, watercress and tomato wedges.

Minted lamb chops make a △ delicious addition to a cold buffet spread.

Colourful Jellied lamb slices are ▷ an interesting new way to serve cold roast lamb. Serve with potato salad.

LANCASHIRE HOT POT

Serves 3–4

**750g (1½lb) middle neck of
    mutton or lamb
2 level teaspoons salt
750g (1½lb) potatoes
2 onions
1 carrot
3 sticks celery
300ml (½ pint) beef stock**

1. Preheat oven to moderate,
180°C (350°F) or gas 4.
2. Wipe and trim the meat of
excess fat. Divide into joints or
cut into pieces and sprinkle with
salt.
3. Prepare the vegetables, slice
the potatoes and cut remaining
vegetables into pieces.
4. Arrange the meat and
vegetables in layers in a
casserole, reserving the potatoes
for the top.
5. Add the stock and top with a
layer of neatly arranged potatoes.
6. Cover with greaseproof paper
and a lid and bake in centre of
oven for 1½ hours. Remove the lid
and paper.
7. Replace in the oven for a
further 30 minutes to brown the
top.

=== **COOK'S TIP** ===

To add more colour, flavour and
thickness to the hot pot, coat the
lamb in well seasoned flour. Fry in
hot oil or dripping to brown and
seal on all sides. Drain and layer
with the vegetables; continue as
recipe.

ORIENTAL LAMB

Serves 4

**50g (2oz) dried apricots, soaked
50g (2oz) breadcrumbs
50g (2oz) ham, chopped
1 egg, beaten
salt and pepper
1 shoulder of lamb or best end
    neck of lamb, boned
50g (2oz) fat
225g (8oz) long-grain rice
2 onions, chopped
1 dessertspoon curry powder
600ml (1 pint) beef stock
slices red and green pepper to
    garnish**

1. Preheat oven to moderate,
180°C (350°F) or gas 4.
2. Combine chopped apricots,
breadcrumbs, ham, egg and
seasoning to make stuffing.
3. Spread on the meat, roll up and
tie firmly.
4. Melt the fat and brown meat
on all sides.
5. Remove and gently fry rice,
onion and curry powder.
6. Add meat and pour stock over.
7. Cover and cook in centre of
oven for 2-2½ hours, adding more
stock, if necessary.
8. Garnish with slices of red and
green pepper.

=== **COOK'S TIP** ===

If your butcher is too busy to bone
a shoulder of lamb for you why not
try doing it yourself? Place on a
firm surface; if using a board, cover
it with a cloth. Use a small, sharp
knife. Before boning, feel all over
the joint to find out where the
bones are located and where they
join. For example, the shoulder has
a large, thin, fan-shaped shoulder
blade. Use firm cutting strokes,
keeping as close to the bone as
possible. Work from the edge to the
inside of the meat, rotating as
necessary. Work from both ends of
one bone if easier. Any extra pieces
of meat adhering to the bone can be
cut off and tucked inside before
rolling.

△ *Lancashire hot pot provides both
meat and vegetables cooked
together and serves as meal on its
own.*

◁ *A tempting entertaining idea,
Oriental lamb is a boned, rolled
shoulder with apricot stuffing.*

LAMB GENEVIEVE

Serves 4

1 kilo (2lb) middle neck of lamb
1 large onion, peeled and
   chopped
750g (1½lb) potatoes, peeled
   and diced
225g (8oz) tomatoes, sliced
600ml (1 pint) stock
salt and pepper
1 small can pimentos, cut into
   strips
1 small packet (225g or 8oz)
   frozen green beans
fresh mint if available

1. Preheat oven to very moderate,
170°C (325°F) or gas 3.
2. Trim meat, cut into chops and
place in a casserole.
3. Add onion, potatoes and
tomatoes, pour in stock and
season with salt and pepper.
4. Cover closely with lid or foil
and cook in centre of oven for
about 2 hours, or until meat is
tender.
5. Stir in pimento and frozen
beans, cover with lid again and
continue cooking for a further 30
minutes.
6. Serve sprinkled with chopped
mint if available.

═══ COOK'S TIP ═══

Frozen beans need to be thawed for
1 hour before use so they can be
broken up and not added to
casserole in one block, as this
would slow down cooking time. A
small can of drained green beans
could be added for last 10 minutes
cooking time in place of frozen
beans.

SWEET SEPTEMBER CASSEROLE

Serves 6

750g (1½lb) lean stewing lamb
2–3 tablespoons salad oil
1 onion, peeled and sliced
25g (1oz) flour
salt and pepper
300ml (½ pint) chicken stock
300ml (½ pint) dry cider
225g (8oz) fresh or canned
   plums or greengages
100g (4oz) carrots

1. Preheat oven to very moderate,
170°C (325°F) or gas 3.
2. Trim meat and cut into small
pieces.
3. Heat oil in a flameproof
casserole and fry onion gently for
2–3 minutes, or until lightly
browned. Remove onion with a
draining spoon and keep on one
side.
4. Toss meat in flour seasoned
with salt and pepper until coated
all over.
5. Add meat to oil remaining in
the casserole and stir over gentle
heat until browned all over.
Sprinkle in any remaining flour
and stir over gentle heat for 1
minute.
6. Remove casserole from heat
and gradually stir in stock,
together with the cider.
7. Return to heat, add prepared
onion and bring to the boil,
stirring. Cover closely with lid or
foil and cook in centre of oven for
about 1½ hours.
8. Add washed, halved and stoned
plums or greengages and return to
oven for a further 20–30 minutes,
or until fruit is tender.
9. Stir in grated carrot just before
serving.

Slow Cooker Method
1. Proceed as stages 2–6 above,
inclusive, but using a saucepan.
2. Return to heat, add prepared
onion and bring to the boil,
stirring.
3. Transfer to a preheated slow
cooker. Cook on High for 30
minutes and on Low for 5 hours.
Add washed, halved and stoned
plums or greengages and continue
cooking 1–2 hours. Stir in grated
carrot just before serving.

A colourful quick to prepare lamb △
casserole, serve Lamb Genevieve for
a midweek family treat.

Sweet September casserole is full of ▷
flavour due to the unusual
ingredient, plums, added to it.

VEAL CACCIATORA

Serves 4–6

15g (½oz) butter
1 medium onion, chopped
1 garlic clove, crushed
 (optional)
750g (1½lb) lean pie veal, cut in
 4cm (1½ inch) cubes
2 green peppers, blanched and
 chopped
1 red pepper, blanched and
 chopped
6 tomatoes, peeled and
 quartered
salt and pepper
150ml (¼ pint) soured cream
2 tablespoons freshly chopped
 parsley, and basil if available

1. Melt butter in pan and fry
onion gently for 3 minutes.
2. Add garlic if liked.
3. Add veal and fry gently for a
further 3 minutes.
4. Stir in peppers and tomatoes
and bring gently to boil, stirring
continuously.
5. Season, cover and simmer
gently for 1½ hours, until veal is
cooked.
6. Before serving, stir in soured
cream and herbs and reheat
without boiling.
7. Serve with plain boiled rice.

OSSO BUCO

Serves 4

1 kilo (2lb) shin of veal, cut into
 four pieces
25g (1oz) flour
salt
freshly ground black pepper
4 tablespoons olive oil
1 garlic clove, peeled and
 crushed
1 medium onion, peeled and
 chopped
2 carrots, peeled and sliced
150ml (¼ pint) dry white wine
150ml (¼ pint) stock or water
2–3 tablespoons tomato purée
1 bouquet garni
grated rind of half a lemon
finely chopped parsley

1. Preheat oven to moderate,
180°C (350°F) or gas 4.
2. Toss pieces of veal in flour
seasoned with salt and pepper.
3. Heat olive oil in a flameproof
casserole, add meat and cook
until browned all over.
4. Stir in garlic, onion, carrots,
wine and stock or water. Blend in
tomato purée and add bouquet
garni.
5. Cover closely with lid or foil
and cook in centre of oven for
about 1½ hours, or until meat is
tender.
6. Remove bouquet garni and
serve sprinkled with lemon rind
and finely chopped parsley.

===== COOK'S TIP =====

This recipe adapts easily for use in
a slow cooker or pressure cooker.
For the slow cooker, complete
stages 2–4 in the recipe, but using
a saucepan. Transfer to a preheated
slow cooker and cook on High for
30 minutes and Low for about 6
hours. Complete recipe as in stage
6.

 For the pressure cooker, follow
stages 2–4 of the recipe, using the
cooker itself as a saucepan. Cover,
bring to High pressure, lower heat
and cook for 15 minutes. Reduce
pressure and remove the lid.
Remove bouquet garni, thicken if
liked, and serve as stage 6 of the
recipe.

△ *Try serving Italian Veal
Cacciatora with saffron-flavoured
rice and a green salad.*

◁ *Osso buco is a satisfying veal
casserole which originated in Italy.*

PAPRIKA VEAL

Serves 4

500g (1lb) stewing veal
25g (1oz) butter
1 large onion, peeled and
  chopped
1–2 level teaspoons mild
  paprika pepper
1 level tablespoon tomato
  purée
400ml (¾ pint) chicken stock
salt
freshly ground black pepper
175g (6oz) long-grain rice
1 small carton yogurt or soured
  cream
chopped parsley
finely grated rind of half a
  lemon

1. Preheat oven to very moderate, 170°C (325°F) or gas 3.
2. Trim meat and cut into neat cubes.
3. Melt butter in a frying pan and fry meat until golden brown all over. Transfer to a casserole, using a draining spoon.
4. Add onion to fat remaining in the pan and fry gently until tender.
5. Stir in paprika pepper and tomato purée, then gradually blend in the stock. Season with salt and pepper, then pour over veal in casserole.
6. Cover closely with lid or foil and cook in centre of oven for about 1 hour, then stir in the rice.
7. Replace lid or foil and continue cooking for a further 30 minutes, or until rice is cooked and meat is tender.
8. Stir in yogurt or soured cream, reserving a little.
9. Pour rest of yogurt or soured cream on top and serve sprinkled with a little chopped parsley and finely grated lemon rind.

═══ COOK'S TIP ═══

This is another recipe ideal for cooking in a slow cooker. Follow stages 2–5 of the recipe, using the slow cooker instead of the casserole. Cook on High for 30 minutes and Low for 6 hours. Cook rice in a separate saucepan, drain, add to slow cooker and cook on Low for a further 15 minutes. Complete recipe as described in stages 8 and 9.

HUNTER'S VEAL

Serves 4

4 thin slices of veal
salt and pepper
50g (2oz) butter
1 onion, finely chopped
1 garlic clove, crushed
50g (2oz) mushroom stalks,
  chopped
1–2 tablespoons white wine or
  cooking sherry
150ml (¼ pint) brown gravy
1 good tablespoon tomato
  purée

1. Season veal, melt butter in a frying pan and cook meat quickly on both sides.
2. Remove from pan and fry onion, garlic and mushroom stalks until tender.
3. Add wine or sherry, gravy and tomato purée.
4. Replace meat and simmer gently for about 10 minutes.
5. Serve with boiled spaghetti.

═══ COOK'S TIP ═══

Slices of veal are often called escalopes. Allow one per person. To tenderize each slice, put it between two pieces of greaseproof paper and pound it gently with a meat tenderizer or the end of a wooden rolling pin. Remove from paper and cook as directed.

A complete meal, spicy Veal △ paprika is cooked with rice and topped with yogurt or soured cream.

For a dinner party, serve Hunter's ▷ veal with buttered noodles and whole French beans.

BARBECUED SPARE RIBS

Serves 6

It is perfectly all right to leave the chops marinating in the sauce all day before they are roasted. Make sure they are in a china dish and are left in a cool place.

1.5 kilo (3lb) spare ribs
900ml (1½ pints) water
4 tablespoons vinegar
3 tablespoons soya sauce
3 tablespoons clear honey
3 tablespoons plum or apricot jam
2 teaspoons Worcestershire sauce
1½ teaspoons made mustard
2 tablespoons lemon juice
1 tablespoon tomato ketchup

1. Preheat oven to moderate, 180°C (350°F) or gas 4.
2. Remove the rind and any excess fat from the meat then cut it into chops between the bones, if necessary.
3. Cut each chop in half for ease of eating.
4. Put the meat into a large pan with the water and 2 tablespoons of the vinegar.
5. Bring to the boil then reduce the heat and simmer the chops for 15 minutes.
6. Drain the chops and place them in a roasting tin.
7. In a pan, mix the soya sauce with the honey, the remaining vinegar, the jam, Worcestershire sauce, mustard, lemon juice and tomato ketchup.
8. Place over a gentle heat until the ingredients are well blended.
9. Pour the sauce over the chops then cook in the centre of the oven for 40 minutes, basting them occasionally.
10. Increase the oven heat to moderately hot, 200°C (400°F) or gas 6, for 15 minutes to brown the chops. Serve in a large dish.

PORK CHOPS TROPICALE

Serves 4

4 pork chops
25g (1oz) lard
300ml (½ pint) orange juice
2 tablespoons powdered ginger
1 teaspoon salt
pepper
¼ teaspoon Tabasco sauce
1 tablespoon cornflour
1 tablespoon water
4 pineapple slices, halved
4 slices orange

1. Preheat oven to moderate, 180°C (350°F) or gas 4.
2. Brown chops on both sides in fat, then transfer to a casserole.
3. Mix orange juice with sugar, ginger, salt, pepper and Tabasco and pour over the chops.
4. Bake in centre of oven for about an hour.
5. Place the drained chops on a hot serving dish and keep warm.
6. Mix cornflour and water with meat juices and cook until sauce has boiled and thickened.
7. Garnish chops with pineapple and orange slices and pour sauce over.
8. Serve with creamed potatoes.

=== **COOK'S TIP** ===

Many oriental dishes use fresh root ginger. It has a clean, almost lemon taste and is not as hot as expected. Fresh ginger can be bought in some supermarkets and specialist shops. It is knobbly, and beige in colour. Buy about 100g (4oz) – it will keep for a week or so in the refrigerator. Peel one large knob and chop enough to make 1 tablespoon. Use in place of powdered ginger.

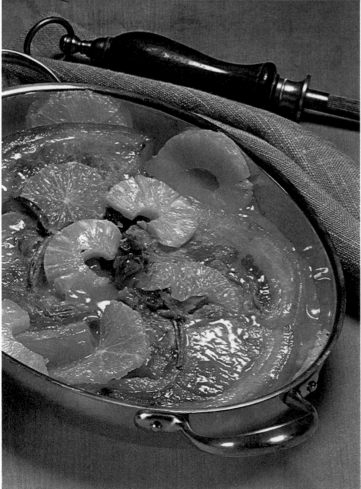

△ *Barbecued spare ribs can be served as a tangy main course or as part of a party spread.*

◁ *Pork combines well with fruit; attractive Pork chops tropicale is flavoured with orange and pineapple.*

PORK AND APPLE KEBABS

Serves 2

350g (12oz) pork fillet or 2 pork chops
1 cooking apple
4 streaky bacon rashers
6 bayleaves
25g (1oz) butter, melted

1. Light the grill.
2. Remove the meat from the bones if using chops then cut the meat into 16 pieces.
3. Peel, core and cut the apple in eight.
4. De-rind the bacon and stretch the rashers with the back of a knife, then cut each one in half.
5. Wrap a piece of bacon around each piece of apple.
6. Thread the pieces on to two kebab skewers in the order of pork, apple, pork, bayleaf, until all pieces are used.
7. Brush the kebabs with butter and grill for 3 minutes on either side then turn the grill down and continue to cook for 20 minutes, turning them again half way through the cooking.
8. Serve with mushroom pilaff.

MUSHROOM PILAFF

Serves 2

1 medium onion
50g (2oz) mushrooms
25g (1oz) margarine
100g (4oz) long-grain rice
300ml (½ pint) stock
salt and pepper

1. Peel and finely slice the onion.
2. Trim the mushrooms, then slice them finely.
3. Melt the margarine, add the onion and cook for 5 minutes until soft but not coloured.
4. Add the rice and fry until opaque.
5. Stir in the mushrooms with the stock.
6. Bring to the boil, reduce the heat, cover and simmer for 20–25 minutes, until the rice is tender.
7. Check for seasoning.

PORK PEKING

Serves 4–6

750g (1½lb) lean stewing pork
3 tablespoons oil
2 onions, peeled and sliced
25g (1oz) flour
salt and pepper
300ml (½ pint) water
1 green pepper, de-seeded and sliced
1 small can mandarin oranges
1 tablespoon vinegar
little soy sauce
1 chicken stock cube
1 can (87g or 3½oz) pimento, drained and cut into strips

1. Preheat oven to very moderate, 170°C (325°F) or gas 3.
2. Trim meat and cut into cubes.
3. Heat oil in a flameproof casserole and fry onions until lightly browned. Remove from pan with a draining spoon and keep on one side.
4. Toss meat in flour seasoned with salt and pepper and fry in fat remaining in the casserole, until brown all over.
5. Sprinkle in any remaining flour and stir over gentle heat for 1 minute.
6. Remove casserole from heat and gradually blend in water. Add cooked onion, green pepper, liquid drained from mandarin oranges, vinegar, soy sauce and chicken stock cube.
7. Return to heat, bring to the boil and simmer gently for 2 minutes, stirring continuously.
8. Cover closely with lid or foil and cook in centre of oven for about 1½ hours.
9. Add mandarin oranges and pimento and continue cooking for a further 10–15 minutes, or until meat is tender.

═══ COOK'S TIP ═══

All meat for stewing should be cut across the grain for tender meat. The grain is the long sinew of the muscle and by cutting across and not with the grain, it ensures softening and quicker cooking. For this reason, try to buy stewing meat in one piece and cut up yourself as the grain is more easily recognizable if the meat is in one piece.

Pork and apple kebabs with Mushroom pilaff make a colourful dinner party main course. Serve with salad. △

Pork Peking, flavoured with mandarin oranges, is cooked slowly in a piquant sweet and sour sauce. ▷

PINEAPPLE PORK CHOPS

Serves 4

50g (2oz) lard or a little oil
4 thick pork chops
1 garlic clove
1 medium can pineapple rings
20g ($\frac{3}{4}$oz) cornflour
1 tablespoon tomato purée
1 bayleaf
1 stick celery, chopped
1 sprig of parsley
1 sprig of thyme
salt and pepper
1 small onion, chopped

1. Preheat oven to moderate, 180°C (350°F) or gas 4.
2. Melt the lard or oil in a pan. Fry the pork chops until brown on each side but not cooked through.
3. Put into a casserole which has been rubbed round with a clove of garlic.
4. Top each chop with a pineapple ring and reserve the juice.
5. Blend the pineapple juice with the cornflour and tomato purée.
6. Add bayleaf, celery, parsley and thyme.
7. Season very well and add the onion.
8. Pour over the pork and cover the casserole with a well fitting lid.
9. Put in centre of oven for 1½ hours. Take off the lid for the last 20 minutes.
10. Serve with new potatoes garnished with chopped parsley, and a green salad.

===== COOK'S TIP =====

Pork chops with fruit have been combined not just for flavour but also for easy digestion. Roast pork and apple sauce is another example. The richness of the pork is made more palatable by the tartness of fruit such as pineapple. For an alternative use rings of apple. Core a cooking apple but do not peel. Cut into 2.5cm (1 inch) slices and place a slice on top of each chop. Use 150ml (¼ pint) stock or water in place of pineapple juice.

STUFFED BELLY OF PORK

Serves 4

1 kilo (2lb) belly of pork, boned
50g (2oz) white breadcrumbs
25g (1oz) shredded suet
25g (1oz) sultanas
½ teaspoon mixed herbs
1 small egg, beaten
50g (2oz) redcurrant jelly
1 can (187g or 7½oz) apple purée or 1 large cooking apple cooked with very little water

1. Preheat oven to moderately hot, 200°C (400°F) or gas 6.
2. Trim off excess fat from the meat. Score the skin.
3. Make stuffing by mixing breadcrumbs, suet, sultanas, and herbs together. Bind with egg.
4. Spread stuffing over the meat. Roll up and secure with string.
5. Wrap pork in foil and place in a roasting tin in oven for 30 minutes.
6. Lower temperature to 180°C (350°F) or gas 4 and cook a further 1¾ hours.
7. Remove foil. Return to oven for 15 minutes to brown and crisp skin.
8. Make sauce by melting redcurrant jelly and adding apple purée. Heat through and serve separately.
9. Garnish with watercress and serve at once.

===== COOK'S TIP =====

This recipe uses one of the more economical joints of pork and needs to be well cooked. Use a transparent roasting bag in place of foil if liked. This keeps in all the juices but still browns the meat.

△ *Pineapple pork chops are an exciting new way to dress up pork. Cooking in the oven makes them really tender.*

◁ *Serve delicious, rich Stuffed belly of pork with creamed potatoes.*

RAISED PORK PIE

Serves 4

hot water crust pastry made
   with 350g (12oz) flour (see
   recipe below)
750g (1½lb) pork fillet
salt and pepper
1 level teaspoon sage
1 large egg, beaten
about 5 tablespoons liquid
   aspic jelly, made from a
   packet

1. Preheat oven to moderately
hot. 200°C (400°F) or gas 6.
2. Mould about two-thirds of the
pastry around the base and sides
of a well-greased small pie mould
or a small, deep round cake tin
with loose base (keep rest of
pastry warm, wrapped in foil,
while you do this).
3. Dice the pork and put it in the
pastry-lined tin with seasoning
and herbs.
4. Wet edges of pastry and put
pastry lid in place. Flute edge.
5. Make a fairly large hole in the
centre of the pie.
6. Bake in the centre of the oven,
for 30 minutes then reduce heat to
moderate, 180°C (350°F) or gas 4,
cover top with foil and cook for
another 1 hour. Carefully take pie
out of tin, brush the top and sides
with egg.
7. Put on a baking sheet and cook
for another 20 minutes.
8. Put a funnel in the hole in the
top of the pie and pour in the
liquid aspic. (Make a funnel from
foil.)
9. Leave pie to get cold.

HOT WATER CRUST PASTRY

Makes 350g or 12oz pastry

350g (12oz) plain flour
1½ level teaspoons salt
175g (6oz) lard
3 tablespoons milk
1 large egg, beaten

1. Sift flour and salt into a bowl.
2. Put the lard in a small
saucepan with the milk and 4½
tablespoons cold water.
3. Heat gently until lard has
melted then bring to the boil.
4. Add to flour and beat well.
5. Add enough of the egg to make
a smooth and glossy dough.
6. Use at once and remember to
wrap any pastry waiting to be
shaped in foil to keep it warm.

PORK VINDALOO

Serves 4

500g (1lb) lean pork
1 rounded dessertspoon
   demerara sugar
2 tablespoons vinegar
25g (1oz) dripping or lard
1 large onion, peeled and
   chopped
2 level dessertspoons curry
   powder
1 bayleaf
3 tomatoes, peeled and chopped
salt and pepper

1. Trim and cut pork into small
cubes, place in a bowl and
sprinkle with sugar and vinegar.
2. Leave for about 2 hours,
turning occasionally with a metal
spoon.
3. Preheat oven to very moderate,
170°C (325°F) or gas 3.
4. Melt dripping or lard in a pan,
and fry onion lightly for 2–3
minutes.
5. Stir in prepared pork together
with juices. Add curry powder,
bayleaf, tomatoes, salt and
pepper.
6. Bring to the boil, then transfer
to a casserole and cover closely
with lid or foil.
7. Cook in centre of oven for 1½–2
hours, or until meat is tender.
8. Serve with boiled rice and
sliced bananas tossed in lemon
juice.

=== **COOK'S TIP** ===

Be sure to adjust seasoning after
the meat is cooked as dishes with
curry powder also need plenty of
salt.

*A Raised pork pie is impressive △
summertime fare to serve with
salad. Ideal for picnics, too.*

*Spicy Pork vindaloo can be made ▷
using beef or lamb. Serve with side
dishes, like cucumber and yogurt.*

RIVIERA CASSEROLE

Serves 6–8

**1.5 kilo (3lb) smoked bacon
  joint
4 black peppercorns
1 bayleaf
whole cloves
2 tablespoons honey
50g (2oz) butter
225g (8oz) onions, peeled and
  chopped
500g (1lb) tomatoes, peeled and
  sliced
2 garlic cloves, peeled and
  crushed
1 level teaspoon sweet basil
salt and pepper**

1. Soak bacon overnight in cold water to cover.
2. Drain joint and place in a saucepan with fresh, cold water to cover. Add peppercorns and bayleaf. Bring to the boil and simmer gently for 1 hour.
3. Preheat oven to moderately hot, 190°C (375°F) or gas 5.
4. Remove bacon joint from the saucepan, carefully strip off skin, score fat and stud with cloves. Place in a casserole and pour honey over top.
5. Melt butter in a frying pan and fry onions gently until tender, then stir in tomatoes, garlic and basil. Season well to taste with salt and pepper, then pour around bacon in the casserole.
6. Cover closely with lid or foil and cook in centre of oven for 25 minutes. Remove lid or foil and continue cooking for a further 15 minutes, or until bacon is tender.

CALIFORNIAN PLATTER

Serves 6

**6 bacon chops
3 red dessert apples
1 can (850g or 1lb 14oz) fruit
  cocktail
1 lemon, thinly sliced
1 level tablespoon cornflour
1 tablespoon water**

1. Preheat oven to moderate, 180°C (350°F) or gas 4.
2. Trim a little fat from the bacon chops and heat it gently in a pan until it begins to run.
3. Remove the pieces of fat and fry bacon chops until golden brown on both sides. Drain well and transfer to a shallow casserole.
4. Wash, core and halve apples and place half an apple on top of each chop.
5. Cover closely with lid or foil and cook in centre of oven for about 45 minutes.
6. Meanwhile, drain fruit cocktail and pour the syrup into the pan in which the chops were cooked. Add sliced lemon and boil until liquid is reduced to about a teacupful.
7. Stir in cornflour blended with water and simmer gently until thick and clear, stirring continuously. Stir in the fruit.
8. Remove cover from casserole and pour fruit sauce over chops. Leave uncovered and continue cooking for a further 15 minutes, or until heated through.
9. Serve with freshly boiled rice.

═══ COOK'S TIP ═══

If you cannot buy bacon chops perhaps you could have the butcher cut some, about 2cm (about ¾ inch) thick, from a side of back bacon.

Alternatively, use thick ham steaks cut in two pieces in the recipe. Use 2 tablespoons lard or dripping for frying the ham before transferring to a baking dish.

△ *Riviera casserole is a smoked bacon joint casseroled whole with onions, tomatoes and garlic.*

◁ *Bacon, apples and fruit cocktail blend together perfectly to make attractive California platter.*

GAMMON OR HAM AND ORANGE

Serves 4

4 slices gammon or thick slices
   ham
2 tablespoons marmalade
25g (1oz) brown sugar
2 oranges

1. Preheat the grill. Trim the rind
from the gammon and snip the fat;
brush one side of each piece with
some marmalade.
2. Sprinkle with some brown
sugar and grill for 5 minutes.
3. Turn the slices, put rest of
marmalade and sugar on the
second side.
4. Grill for a further 5–6 minutes,
until the gammon is cooked.
5. Peel and slice the oranges and
serve with the gammon.

══ COOK'S TIP ══

Gammon and ham are often sold in
individual circular steaks or
serving pieces. These rings are
sometimes held together with a
plastic coating so be sure to remove
this before cooking.

Cranberry sauce is a good
alternative to marmalade and can
be used in the same way in this
recipe.

SUGARED HAM

Serves 4

1 can (1 kilo or 2lb) ham
25g (1oz) demerara sugar
15g (½oz) cloves
1 can peach halves
1 small can prunes
1 lettuce

1. Preheat oven to hot, 230°C
(450°F) or gas 8.
2. Remove ham from the can and
sprinkle thickly with demerara
sugar.
3. Stud with cloves and put in a
small roasting tin.
4. Bake in centre of oven for
approximately 10 minutes, until
sugar turns golden brown.
5. Turn oven temperature down
to very cool, 120°C (250°F) or gas
½, and leave ham in oven for a
further 20 minutes.
6. Drain peaches and prunes,
then stone prunes.
7. Place ham on a bed of lettuce
on a serving dish and surround
with peach halves and prunes.

══ COOK'S TIP ══

Ham prepared this way is delicious
and the finish can be used on any
cooked ham or bacon joint. When
using canned ham make a 'collar'
to preserve the shape for easier
carving. To do this use a doubled
strip of greaseproof paper or foil
the same height as the meat. Wrap
round and secure with a wooden
cocktail stick. Remove after
cooking.

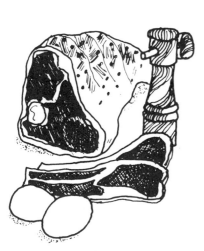

Gammon or ham and orange blend △
well together to create a speedy
main course with a difference.

When unexpected guests arrive, ▷
Sugared ham can be made almost
completely from the store cupboard.

BACON AND ONION PUDDING

Serves 4

piece boiling bacon (about 500g or 1lb)
suet crust pastry made with 225g (8oz) flour (see Basic recipes, page 7)
1 medium onion, skinned and sliced
salt and pepper
1 level teaspoon sage
parsley to garnish

1. Leave bacon to soak overnight in cold water.
2. Next day, drain bacon and cut into large cubes.
3. Use two-thirds of the pastry to line a 1-litre (1½- or 2-pint) pudding basin.
4. Fill the pastry-lined basin with layers of onion, seasoning, sage and bacon.
5. Pour in about 150ml (¼ pint) water.
6. Wet edges of pastry in the basin.
7. Roll out rest of pastry to make a lid for pudding and put in position.
8. Cover with greaseproof paper then with foil.
9. Boil or steam for 3 hours.
10. Garnish with parsley, if liked.

=== **COOK'S TIP** ===

An excellent variation on an old favourite, steak and kidney pudding. To line the basin with suet pastry, roll pastry out to a circle not more than 1cm (½ inch) thick. Cut out ¼ of mixture in a wedge and reserve for the top. Dampen the two cut edges of pastry and arrange in the bowl, pressing these edges together. Press pastry down into bowl well, fill, reroll reserved pastry into a circle to fit the top.

SAUSAGEMEAT BALLS WITH SPANISH RICE

Serves 4

500g (1lb) sausagemeat
50g (2oz) flour, seasoned with salt and pepper
fat for frying
175g (6oz) long-grain rice
50g (2oz) lard
1 onion, chopped
1 small green pepper, chopped
2 sticks celery, chopped
1 small can tomatoes

1. Roll the sausagemeat into seven or eight balls and then roll in a little seasoned flour. Fry on all sides.
2. Boil the rice in plenty of salted water for about 10–15 minutes, until tender, then drain it.
3. Melt the lard in a pan, stir in the onion, pepper and celery and cook gently for about 15 minutes.
4. Add tomatoes, season well and, when hot, stir in the rice.
5. Heat through and serve on a hot dish.
6. Arrange the sausagemeat balls on the top.

=== **COOK'S TIP** ===

Sausagemeat is convenient for this recipe but sausages could be removed from their skins and used instead. If preparing the meat balls earlier, leave in the refrigerator and dredge with a little extra flour before frying. This will keep the balls a good shape and prevent them breaking up in the pan. Add 1 tablespoon chilli powder to the rice with the tomatoes and call it Mexican rice.

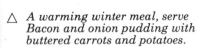

△ *A warming winter meal, serve Bacon and onion pudding with buttered carrots and potatoes.*

◁ *Colourful Sausagemeat balls with Spanish rice are a popular choice with children.*

COTTAGE CASEROLE

Serves 4–6

1 rabbit (about 1.5 kilo or 3lb),
   cut into joints
40g (1½oz) flour
salt
freshly ground black pepper
50g (2oz) dripping
1 large leek, washed and sliced
2 teaspoons yeast extract
600ml (1 pint) chicken stock or
   water
2 carrots, peeled and sliced
1 stick celery, cleaned and
   chopped
1 bayleaf
2 tablespoons tomato ketchup
dash of Worcestershire sauce
chopped parsley to garnish

1. Preheat oven to moderate,
180°C (350°F) or gas 4.
2. Toss rabbit joints in flour
seasoned with salt and pepper.
3. Melt dripping in a pan and fry
rabbit joints until golden brown
all over. Transfer to a casserole
using a draining spoon.
4. Add leek to fat remaining in
the pan and fry gently for 2–3
minutes.
5. Sprinkle in any remaining
flour and stir over gentle heat for
1 minute.
6. Remove pan from heat. Stir in
yeast extract, then gradually
blend in stock or water.
7. Return to heat, bring to the
boil and simmer for 2 minutes,
stirring continuously.
8. Add carrots, celery, bayleaf,
tomato ketchup and
Worcestershire sauce. Stir well
together, then pour over rabbit in
casserole.
9. Cover closely with lid or foil
and cook in centre of oven for
about 2 hours, or until rabbit is
tender.
10. Remove bayleaf and sprinkle
with parsley before serving.

OLD ENGLISH CASEROLE

Serves 4

225g (8oz) butter beans
25g (1oz) butter
1 large oxtail, cut into joints
2 onions, peeled and chopped
25g (1oz) flour
400ml (¾ pint) stock
good pinch of marjoram
1 bayleaf
2 carrots, peeled and sliced
2 teaspoons lemon juice
salt and pepper

1. Soak the butter beans
overnight in cold water to cover.
2. Preheat oven to moderately
hot, 190°C (375°F) or gas 5.
3. Melt butter in a frying pan and
fry oxtail until golden brown,
then transfer to a casserole.
4. Fry onions in fat remaining in
the frying pan for 2–3 minutes,
then add to meat in the casserole.
5. Sprinkle flour into fat
remaining in the pan and stir over
gentle heat for 2–3 minutes.
6. Remove pan from heat and
gradually blend in stock.
7. Return to heat, bring to the
boil, stirring, then pour over the
meat.
8. Add well drained butter beans,
marjoram, bayleaf, carrots and
lemon juice. Season well with salt
and pepper.
9. Cover closely with lid or foil
and cook in centre of oven for 30
minutes.
10. Reduce oven temperature to
cool, 150°C (300°F) or gas 2 and
cook for a further 2½–3 hours, or
until meat is tender.

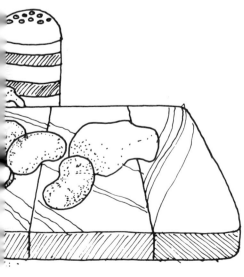

For a change, try flavoursome △
Cottage casserole – rabbit braised
slowly with vegetables.

Old English casserole contains ▷
oxtail which always provides an
excellent flavoured dish.

STUFFED CALF'S LIVER A TRANSMONTANA

Serves 4

500g (1lb) calf's liver, sliced
3 hard-boiled eggs, sliced
150g (5oz) lean smoked ham
1 garlic clove, crushed
1 sprig parsley
1 teaspoon salt and freshly ground pepper
50g (2oz) butter
1 medium onion, chopped
3 egg yolks
juice of half a lemon

1. Preheat oven to moderately hot, 190°C (375°F) or gas 5.
2. Place on each slice of liver, equal portions of egg, chopped ham, a little garlic, chopped parsley, salt and pepper.
3. Roll up the liver round its filling and skewer or tie with string.
4. Heat the butter in a frying pan and fry the onion until tender. Add 3 tablespoons water.
5. Place the liver in a baking tin or dish and pour over the onion mixture and cook in the centre of the oven for 15–20 minutes.
16. Remove from the oven, cover with scrambled eggs, made with the egg yolks and the lemon juice.

FAMILY CASSEROLE

Serves 4

500g (1lb) lamb's liver
50g (2oz) butter
4 back bacon rashers, trimmed and cut into small pieces
1 onion, peeled and sliced
50g (2oz) flour
salt
freshly ground black pepper
600ml (1 pint) beef stock
2 tomatoes, peeled and chopped
100g (4oz) button mushrooms, washed, trimmed and chopped
3 sticks celery, washed and chopped

1. Preheat oven to moderate, 180°C (350°F) or gas 4.
2. Cut liver into 2.5cm (1 inch) strips.
3. Melt butter in a frying pan and fry bacon and onion for 4–5 minutes, or until lightly browned. Remove from pan with a draining spoon and transfer to a casserole.
4. Toss liver in flour seasoned with salt and pepper, then fry in fat remaining in the pan until browned on both sides. Transfer to casserole.
5. Sprinkle in any remaining flour and stir over gentle heat for 1 minute.
6. Remove pan from heat and gradually blend in stock.
7. Return to heat, bring to the boil and simmer for 2 minutes, stirring continuously. Add contents of pan to the casserole.
8. Add tomatoes, mushrooms and celery and more seasoning if necessary.
9. Cover closely with lid or foil and cook in centre of oven for about 45 minutes, or until meat is tender.

=== **COOK'S TIP** ===

Since liver is such an excellent source of iron for the diet, it is important to prepare it carefully. Remove the outside skin before use. It is a thin skin hardly noticeable until cooked. If the butcher has sliced the liver the skin may not have been removed beforehand. Have a piece of paper towel handy to wipe knife and fingers when removing skin, and if really slippery dip fingers in a little salt first.

△ *Stuffed calf's liver a transmontana is an unusual yet traditional Portuguese way of serving liver.*

◁ *Instead of frying your liver and bacon, try cooking it slowly in the oven as in Family casserole.*

BRAISED LIVER CASSEROLE

Serves 4

500g (1lb) liver
40g (1½oz) flour
50g (2oz) dripping
3 onions, chopped
4 bacon rashers, chopped
2 carrots, sliced
1 stick celery, chopped
600ml (1 pint) stock

1. Preheat oven to moderate, 180°C (350°F) or gas 4.
2. Slice and flour the liver and fry it in dripping with the onions and bacon.
3. Remove from the pan and keep hot. Fry carrots and celery.
4. Turn all ingredients into a casserole.
5. Season and add stock.
6. Cook in centre of oven for 45 minutes.
7. Serve with creamed potato.

=== COOK'S TIP ===

The careful preparation of liver is discussed in the previous recipe.

CREAMED KIDNEYS WITH PASTA

Serves 4

225g (8oz) pasta shapes
65g (2½oz) butter
1 onion, finely chopped
8 lamb's kidneys
15g (½oz) flour
100g (4oz) mushrooms, sliced
3 tablespoons sharp sauce or chutney
½ beef stock cube dissolved in 400ml (¾ pint) water
salt and pepper
2 tablespoons single or double cream

1. Cook pasta in plenty of boiling, salted water for 10–15 minutes.
2. Melt 40g (1½oz) butter in a pan. Fry onion gently until soft.
3. Meanwhile skin, core and slice kidneys.
4. Toss in flour and add to onions with mushrooms.
5. Fry, turning frequently for 3 minutes. Add sauce, stock, salt and pepper. Bring to boil, stirring.
6. Cook for 2 minutes, then stir in almost all the cream.
7. Toss drained pasta in remaining butter.
8. Pile pasta around kidney mixture. Pour remaining cream over the top and serve at once.

=== COOK'S TIP ===

For a really special supper dish, add ½ teaspoon curry powder to the flour for coating the kidneys. Replace 2 tablespoons water with sherry or red wine. This is a quick dish to prepare so it can be made up at the last minute.

Braised liver casserole may be △
served with white or brown rice
and a green vegetable.

For an attractive, low cost dinner ▷
party dish, try Creamed kidneys
with pasta.

MUSHROOMS AND KIDNEYS WITH DUMPLINGS

Serves 4

500g (1lb) kidneys
1 teaspoon chopped onion
50g (2oz) dripping
600ml (1 pint) stock
100g (4oz) mushrooms, sliced
4 bacon rashers
salt and pepper
1 level teaspoon chopped fresh herbs
150g (5oz) self-raising flour
50g (2oz) shredded suet

1. Skin and core the kidneys and cut into small dice.
2. Cook the onion in the dripping until it is tender.
3. Remove from the pan and add the kidney. Brown in the fat.
4. Add the stock and the mushrooms, onion and chopped bacon. Mix in the seasoning and the herbs.
5. Simmer for 20 minutes.
6. Mix the flour with the suet in a bowl and season well.
7. Blend with a little cold water to make dumplings. Shape into four dumplings and set on top of the stew.
8. Cover with a lid and simmer for a further 20 minutes.

=== **COOK'S TIP** ===

Kidneys from pork, beef or lamb can all be used in cooking. Pork and beef have a stronger flavour and require more cooking time than lamb's kidneys. This makes them ideally suited for stews and casseroles. Combine with cubes of ham or sausagemeat balls to tempt a family reluctant to try a full kidney dish.

KIDNEY AND ONION STEW

Serves 4–6

2 ox kidneys
50g (2oz) flour
salt and pepper
2 medium onions, peeled and sliced
1 tablespoon chopped parsley
½ level teaspoon sweet basil
600ml (1 pint) beef stock

1. Preheat oven to moderate, 180°C (350°F) or gas 4.
2. Skin each kidney, cut in half and remove core. Cut into small pieces then toss in flour seasoned with salt and pepper.
3. Arrange kidneys in a casserole together with onion, parsley, basil and stock.
4. Cover closely with lid or foil and cook in centre of oven for 1½– 2 hours, or until meat is tender.
5. Serve with jacket baked potatoes and baked tomatoes.

△ *Mushrooms and kidneys with dumplings provides a nourishing and filling meal on a cold winter's day.*

◁ *The addition of a few herbs transforms homely Kidney and onion stew.*

Poultry dishes

Poultry has become a regular food in our diets today and here are some new and exciting ways to serve it, including chicken with herbs, spices and fruit. Now turkey can be bought all the year round and most chicken recipes can be substituted with turkey. There are casseroles and all kinds of family dishes, with a good selection of entertaining recipes for special occasions.

CHICKEN CHASSEUR MARENGO

Serves 4

4 chicken breasts
25g (1oz) butter
1 tablespoon oil
2 shallots or small onions,
finely chopped
15g (½oz) flour
2 tablespoons dry sherry
300ml (½ pint) chicken stock
2 level tablespoons tomato
purée
100g (4oz) button mushrooms,
sliced
2 teaspoons lemon juice
seasoning
croûtons to garnish

1. Fry chicken breasts in the butter and oil for 15 minutes, or until cooked through.
2. Drain and keep warm on a serving dish.
3. Fry the shallots or onions in the pan, stir in the flour and blend in the remaining ingredients.
4. Bring to the boil, stirring, and simmer for 10 minutes.
5. Adjust seasoning and pour sauce over chicken.
6. Garnish with croûtons and serve with boiled rice.

=== **COOK'S TIP** ===

The mixture of butter and oil used for frying in this recipe is to prevent the butter from burning. Care must be taken to see the heat is not too high as the chicken must be cooked through.

Add the croûton garnish just at serving time or it will soften and not provide the texture contrast intended. If making this dish to freeze, parcel the croûtons separately and put round the dish at cooking time. Many casseroles are enhanced by serving croûtons or triangles of fried bread as they give something to crunch and chew along with the softer meat and vegetables.

SPICED CHICKEN

Serves 4

4 chicken breasts
25g (1oz) butter
1 tablespoon cooking oil
1 small onion, chopped
15g (½oz) flour
salt and pepper
½ level teaspoon ground ginger
1 level teaspoon paprika
400ml (¾ pint) cider
1 tablespoon tomato purée
¼ teaspoon sugar
1 tablespoon chopped parsley

1. Preheat oven to very moderate, 170°C (325°F) or gas 3.
2. Fry chicken in butter and oil till browned.
3. Remove and fry onion till soft.
4. Work in flour, seasonings, ginger and paprika.
5. Add cider and stir in tomato purée, sugar and parsley.
6. Return chicken to the pan, baste well, cover and simmer for 20 minutes or cook in the oven for 30 minutes.
7. Remove chicken from pan and place on lettuce on a serving dish. Stir sauce well then pour into a sauceboat.
8. Serve chicken with the sauce and boiled rice.

=== **COOK'S TIP** ===

To remove chicken breasts from a whole chicken, cut along one side of the breast bone with a sharp knife. Work cleanly down close to the carcass to loosen the breast in one piece. Turn the bird round and cut the second chicken breast in the same way.

△ *Serve famous Chicken chasseur Marengo for a dinner party accompanied with brocolli or salad.*

◁ *Spiced chicken cooked in cider is a tasty new way to serve chicken. Dry cider is the best choice.*

COQ AU VIN

Serves 4

75g (3oz) butter
2 tablespoons oil
100g (4oz) streaky bacon, trimmed and cut into small pieces
12 button onions, peeled
2 garlic cloves, peeled and crushed
4 chicken pieces
3 tablespoons Cognac
1 bayleaf
6 peppercorns
few stalks parsley
300ml (½ pint) chicken stock
300ml (½ pint) red wine
1 level teaspoon sugar
100g (4oz) button mushrooms, washed
few sprigs of watercress

1. Preheat oven to very moderate, 170°C (325°F) or gas 3.
2. Heat half the butter and the oil in a large frying pan and fry bacon, onions and garlic for 8–10 minutes, or until lightly browned. Remove from the pan with a draining spoon and keep on one side.
3. Add remaining butter to pan and cook chicken pieces for 10 minutes, or until golden brown all over.
4. Remove pan from heat, pour Cognac over and set alight with a match. When flames have died down, transfer chicken and juices in pan to a casserole.
5. Add prepared bacon and onion mixture, bayleaf, peppercorns and parsley to casserole.
6. Pour stock and red wine over and add sugar.
7. Cover closely with lid or foil and cook in centre of oven for about 1 hour.
8. Remove lid, add mushrooms and return to oven for a further 15–20 minutes, or until chicken is tender.
9. Thicken, if liked, with a little cornflour blended with water.
10. Serve garnished with sprigs of watercress.

═══ COOK'S TIP ═══

The two essentials of this well known favourite are brandy and red wine, a change from white wine usually associated and served with poultry.

CLEMENTINE CHICKEN

Serves 6

6 chicken pieces
salt and pepper
1 tablespoon oil
25g (1oz) butter
1 onion, peeled and sliced
25g (1oz) flour
400ml (¾ pint) chicken stock
1 thin-skinned lemon, cut into slices
1 small, thin-skinned orange, cut into slices
2 bayleaves
1 level teaspoon sugar
sprig of watercress

1. Preheat oven to moderately hot, 190°C (375°F) or gas 5.
2. Sprinkle chicken joints with salt and pepper.
3. Heat oil and butter in a frying pan and fry chicken quickly till golden brown. Drain well over pan and transfer to a casserole.
4. Add onion to fat remaining in the pan and cook gently for about 5 minutes, or until tender.
5. Sprinkle in flour and stir over gentle heat for 1 minute.
6. Remove pan from heat and gradually blend in stock.
7. Return to heat, bring to the boil and simmer for 2 minutes, stirring continuously.
8. Add lemon and orange slices and bayleaves. Season with salt, pepper and sugar and pour over chicken.
9. Cover closely with lid or foil and cook in centre of oven for about 45 minutes, or until chicken is tender, removing the lid 15 minutes before end of cooking time to allow top to brown.
10. Serve garnished with watercress.

For a special occasion, serve Coq △ au vin – a classic French dish from Burgundy.

Tangy Clementine chicken is ▷ flavoured with oranges and lemons.

CHICKEN CASEROLE

Serves 4

4 chicken pieces
50g (2oz) plain flour, seasoned
  with salt and pepper
50g (2oz) butter
1 onion, chopped
4 tomatoes, skinned
400ml (¾ pint) chicken stock
2 red peppers, sliced

1. Preheat oven to moderate,
180°C (350°F) or gas 4.
2. Coat chicken pieces in
seasoned flour.
3. Fry on all sides in hot butter
until golden brown. Place in a
casserole.
4. Fry onion in remaining fat.
5. Add with the tomatoes cut into
quarters and chicken stock to the
casserole.
6. Cover and cook in centre of
oven for 1 hour.
7. Add sliced red peppers and
cook for a further 15 minutes.
Serve at once.

===== COOK'S TIP =====

It is possible to buy 'casserole'
chicken. Sometimes labelled
boiling fowl, these are older birds
suitable for long, slow cooking.
When using, cut into pieces – legs,
wings, breast etc. – and use the
carcass to make the stock. The
casserole will require much longer
cooking time (approximately 3
hours in all) and this would be a
good recipe for a slow crock pot
cooker. Alternatively, use a
pressure cooker to soften the
chicken and save time and fuel. Fry
chicken first and then using 2.5cm
(1 inch) chicken stock in bottom of
pressure cooker, cook until almost
tender. Place chicken in casserole
with tomatoes, onions etc. as recipe
to finish cooking.

CIDER CHICKEN AND SWEETCORN

Serves 4

100g (4oz) mushrooms
75g (3oz) butter
1 chicken, cut in pieces
50g (2oz) flour, seasoned with
  salt and pepper
600ml (1 pint) cider
150ml (¼ pint) cream
salt and pepper
1 large can sweetcorn

1. Preheat oven to hot, 230°C
(450°F) or gas 8.
2. Chop mushrooms and fry in 25g
(1oz) butter. Remove from pan.
3. Roll chicken in seasoned flour
and fry in remaining butter until
golden.
4. Place chicken and mushrooms
in a heatproof dish.
5. Boil cider in the frying pan,
stirring with a wooden spoon.
6. Add cream, salt and pepper and
cook for 2 minutes without
boiling.
7. Pour cider sauce over chicken
joints, cover and place in centre
of oven for 30 minutes.
8. Remove chicken to a serving
dish, surround with heated
sweetcorn and pour sauce over.

===== COOK'S TIP =====

Chicken pieces can often be
brought more cheaply frozen than
fresh and in a bag weighing 1.5 kilo
(3lb) or 2.25 kilo (5lb) there will be
a selection of joints. Always thaw
chicken pieces in the refrigerator
or at room temperature before use,
to assess the real size of the pieces
and to carry out any necessary
trimming of excess skin or bone.

△ *Serve quick to prepare Chicken
casserole on busy days. Bake jacket
potatoes at the same time.*

◁ *Flavoursome Cider chicken and
sweetcorn can be served with
creamed or chipped potatoes.*

CRISPY CHICKEN

Serves 4

4 chicken pieces
1 lemon
salt and pepper
2 medium eggs
40g (1½oz) cheese, grated
40g (1½oz) breadcrumbs
fat for deep frying
100g (4oz) mushrooms
25g (1oz) butter
50g (2oz) almonds, toasted
1 lettuce

1. Sprinkle the chicken pieces with lemon juice.
2. Season and leave in a cold place for 2 hours.
3. Dip in beaten egg.
4. Mix together cheese and breadcrumbs and coat the chicken firmly with the mixture.
5. Deep fry until golden. Drain.
6. Fry the sliced mushrooms in the butter and scatter them over the chicken with the almonds.
7. Garnish with lettuce leaves and serve with new potatoes sprinkled with parsley, and peas.

=== COOK'S TIP ===

See note about fresh and frozen chicken under Cider chicken and sweetcorn (opposite). Thawed frozen chicken should be drained well, trimmed and dried in a paper towel before sprinkling with lemon juice. Again this should be well drained before coating otherwise the egg and breadcrumbs will not stick.

CHICKEN COBBLER

Serves 4

4 chicken pieces
salt and pepper
1 level teaspoon thyme
flour to thicken
shortcrust pastry made with 175g (6oz) flour (see Basic recipes, page 7)
1 medium egg, beaten

1. Preheat oven to moderate, 180°C (350°F) or gas 4.
2. Put the chicken pieces in a casserole with just enough water to cover, salt and pepper and thyme.
3. Cover dish and cook for 1½ hours, or until tender.
4. Take chicken meat off the bones.
5. Turn heat up to moderately hot, 200°C (400°F) or gas 6.
6. Thicken the cooking liquid with flour then stir in chicken meat.
7. Put chicken mixture in large, shallow ovenproof dish. Allow to cool.
8. Roll out the pastry to about a 1cm (½ inch) thick and cut out six rounds – just like scones.
9. Put these on top of chicken mixture.
10. Brush pastry with egg.
11. Bake, in centre of preheated oven, for 15–20 minutes, or until golden brown. Serve with asparagus, if liked.

=== COOK'S TIP ===

This recipe can be prepared earlier in the day and the final topping and cooking done at the last minute. It would also be a good way to use up already cooked chicken.

If you do not have fresh chicken stock, use a chicken stock cube in the sauce. Any leftover vegetables such as carrots, beans, peas or sweetcorn could be added to the sauce with the chicken. They give colour and are an alternative to asparagus if it is out of season.

Crispy chicken is coated in cheese △ and breadcrumbs, and then deep fried until golden.

Chicken cobbler is a satisfying ▷ dish to give a hungry family. Choose any favourite vegetable to accompany.

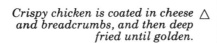

POULET BASQUE

Serves 4

1 dressed chicken (about 1.5 kilo or 3lb)
salt and pepper
3 tablespoons olive oil
2 large green peppers, de-seeded and cut into strips
4 tomatoes, skinned and quartered
100g (4oz) button mushrooms, washed
50g (2oz) lean bacon, cut in small dice
150ml (¼ pint) dry white wine

1. Preheat oven to moderate, 180°C (350°F) or gas 4.
2. Sprinkle chicken with salt and pepper.
3. Heat oil in a large pan and fry chicken until golden brown all over.
4. Transfer chicken to a casserole, draining well.
5. Add green peppers, tomatoes, mushrooms and bacon to pan in which chicken was cooked and fry lightly for 2–3 minutes.
6. Add wine, stir well to remove any sediment around the pan, then pour around chicken in casserole.
7. Cover closely with lid or foil and cook in centre of oven for 30 minutes.
8. Remove cover and continue cooking for a further 30–45 minutes, or until chicken is golden brown and tender.
9. Serve with boiled rice and crisp green salad.

CHICKEN LUAN

Serves 4

100g (4oz) butter or margarine
1 large stick celery, chopped
2–4 level teaspoons curry powder
25g (1oz) flour
2 cans (275g or 10oz) cream of chicken soup
salt and pepper
350g (12oz) cooked chicken, diced
1 can (225g or 8oz) pineapple pieces, drained
225g (8oz) rice
watercress to garnish

1. Melt butter or margarine in a pan. Add celery and curry powder and fry for 3–4 minutes.
2. Add flour and cook for 1 minute.
3. Stir in chicken soup, seasoning, chicken and pineapple and heat gently.
4. Meanwhile, cook rice in boiling, salted water till tender, drain and serve the chicken on it. Garnish with watercress and serve with chutney.

===== COOK'S TIP =====

The flavour of this dish is mainly of curry with a sharpness provided by the pineapple. Since some curry powders are stronger than others use 2 or 3 teaspoons of powder for a more subtle flavour. If pineapple pieces are large, cut in half before adding with the chicken.

△ *Tender Poulet Basque is a whole chicken casseroled in white wine, tomatoes and mushrooms.*

◁ *An interesting way of using cooked chicken, Chicken Luan is flavoured with curry and pineapple.*

CHICKEN ENVELOPE

Serves 2

2 large chicken pieces
salt and pepper
25g (1oz) butter
25g (1oz) flour
2 tablespoons single cream
shortcrust pastry made with
225g (8oz) flour (see Basic
recipes, page 7)
1 medium egg, beaten

1. Put the chicken pieces in a saucepan. Add just enough water to cover and some salt and pepper.
2. Bring to the boil, then cover and simmer for 1 hour, or until meat is tender.
3. Cut the chicken meat off the bones.
4. Reserve 200ml ($\frac{1}{3}$ pint) of the cooking liquid.
5. Melt the butter in a small pan.
6. Stir flour into butter and cook for 2 minutes.
7. Very gradually add the reserved chicken liquid.
8. Bring to the boil, stirring. Cook for 2 minutes, stirring all the time. (This should be a thick sauce.)
9. Stir chicken and cream into the sauce.
10. Add salt and pepper, if it needs more seasoning. Allow to cool.
11. Preheat oven to moderately hot, 200°C (400°F) or gas 6.
12. Roll out the pastry to a large square. Trim neatly.
13. Brush pastry edges with egg.
14. Spoon cooled chicken mixture into centre of pastry.
15. Fold the four corners to the centre to make an envelope. Seal edges well and place on a baking tray.
16. Decorate with pastry half-moons made from the trimmings. Brush with egg.
17. Bake, in the centre of the preheated oven, for 25–30 minutes.
18. If liked, serve with green beans.

CHICKEN VOL-AU-VENT

Serves 3

puff pastry made with 225g
(8oz) flour (see Basic recipes,
page 7)
225g (8oz) cooked chicken
(breast meat)
100g (4oz) green grapes, de-
seeded and halved
50g (2oz) blanched almonds,
lightly toasted
mayonnaise to bind
3 tablespoons double cream
salt and pepper

1. Preheat oven to hot, 220°C (425°F) or gas 7.
2. Roll out the pastry to the size of a bread and butter plate; the pastry must be at least a 1cm ($\frac{1}{2}$ inch) thick. Cut around plate to give neat shape.
3. Using a smaller plate, mark a round in the centre of the pastry, but do not cut right through, just to about a 5mm ($\frac{1}{4}$ inch).
4. Put the pastry on a wetted baking sheet.
5. Bake, in centre of preheated oven, for 15–20 minutes.
6. Remove the pastry lid and any soft bits in the centre.
7. Leave to cool.
8. Chop the pastry lid and put it in the base of the vol-au-vent.
9. Cut the chicken meat into small pieces.
10. Mix chicken with grapes and nuts.
11. Add enough mayonnaise to bind the mixture then stir in the cream. Season.
12. Spoon into the vol-au-vent case and serve at once, with potato croquettes, if liked.

=== **COOK'S TIP** ===

One large vol-au-vent looks very handsome but if you wish to make your pastry case early or freeze for future use, then make individual pastry cases. They would be easier to store and less likely to be damaged than one large one. This recipe is very suitable for frozen puff pastry if time for preparation is short.

Chicken envelope is made with △ shortcrust pastry filled with chicken in creamy sauce.

Elegant Chicken vol-au-vent is ▷ filled with grapes, almonds, cooked chicken and mayonnaise.

TAJ MAHAL CHICKEN

Serves 6

2 teaspoons cooking oil
1 small onion, peeled and finely
    chopped
2 level teaspoons curry powder
½ level teaspoon curry paste
2 tablespoons red wine or wine
    vinegar
juice of ½ lemon
1 level tablespoon apricot jam
300ml (½ pint) mayonnaise (see
    Basic recipes, page 6)
salt and paprika pepper
1 cooked chicken
    (approximately 1.5 kilo or
    3lb)
225g (8oz) long grain rice
French dressing using 2
    tablespoons olive oil (see
    Basic recipes, page 6)
25g (1oz) flaked almonds,
    toasted

1. Heat the oil in a frying pan,
add the onion and fry it gently
until tender but not coloured.
2. Add the curry powder and
paste and cook the mixture for a
few more minutes.
3. Stir in the red wine, lemon
juice and jam and cook all the
ingredients over a brisk heat for
about 3 minutes until they have
reduced.
4. Leave this mixture to cool
completely before stirring it into
the mayonnaise.
5. Check the sauce for seasoning.
6. Remove all the meat from the
chicken and cut it into small
pieces.
7. Cook the rice in boiling, salted
water, for about 12 minutes.
8. Drain the rice thoroughly, then
run cold water through the grains
to separate them and remove
excess starch.
9. Leave the rice to drain for a
little while then turn it into a
bowl and mix in the French
dressing.
10. Arrange around the edge of a
serving dish.
11. Mix the chicken with the
curried mayonnaise and place in
the centre of the rice.
12. Scatter the flaked almonds
over the top.

CURRY MEAL

Serves 4

shortcrust pastry made with
    225g (8oz) flour (see Basic
    recipes, page 7)
175g (6oz) long-grain rice
1 large orange
½ small green pepper
1 small banana
lemon juice
1 level teaspoon curry paste
350g (12oz) leftover cooked
    chicken breast, cut into large
    pieces
25g (1oz) raisins
cucumber slices and lettuce
    leaves to garnish

1. Preheat oven to moderately
hot, 200°C (400°F) or gas 6.
2. Roll out the pastry and use to
line the base and sides of a Swiss
roll tin.
3. Prick pastry with a fork.
4. Bake blind (see page 7) in
centre of preheated oven for 20–25
minutes.
5. Meanwhile, put the rice in a
pan with water to cover.
6. Cook for 20 minutes, or until
all the water is absorbed. Rinse in
cold water, then drain well.
7. While rice is cooking, cut
unpeeled orange into slices.
8. Chop the pepper flesh.
9. Peel and slice banana and toss
it in lemon juice.
10. When the rice is ready, mix in
the curry paste, making sure it is
well blended. Mix in pepper and
banana.
11. Put rice mixture in the cooked
pastry case.
12. Arrange chicken pieces and
raisins on the rice mixture.
13. Garnish with lettuce, orange
and cucumber as shown in the
picture.
14. If liked serve with coconut.

△ *Serve cold curried Taj Mahal
chicken for summer entertaining or
as part of a buffet spread.*

◁ *Attractive Curry meal is a blend of
curried rice, chicken and fruit in a
pastry case.*

VALENCIA PAELLA

Serves 4

4 tablespoons oil
1 large onion, finely chopped
2 red peppers, diced
2 green peppers, diced
2 shallots, finely chopped
1 garlic clove, finely chopped
175g (6oz) mushrooms, sliced
225g (8oz) long-grain rice
pepper, salt and saffron
600ml (1 pint) chicken stock
225–350g (8–12oz) cooked
   chicken, diced
100g (4oz) cooked prawns,
   peeled plus a few unpeeled
   prawns to garnish
1 large onion, cut in rings and
   fried

1. Heat the oil in a large pan.
2. Add the onion, peppers,
shallots and garlic.
3. When the vegetables are soft,
add the mushrooms and heat for
1–2 minutes.
4. Add the rice and cook for 1
minute, stirring continuously.
5. Add pepper, salt and a grain of
saffron.
6. Add the stock gradually, bring
to the boil; stir and lower the heat
to simmer.
7. Cover and cook about 15
minutes, without removing lid or
stirring.
8. Mix in the chicken, cover and
cook for a further 5 minutes.
9. Add prawns and mix well.
10. Turn into casserole dish or
paella pan and garnish with
previously fried onion rings, and
whole, unpeeled prawns.

=== COOK'S TIP ===

This is one recipe where using olive
oil rather than any other cooking
oil would be worth the extra
expense. It adds an essential
flavour to the dish and if you buy a
small bottle keep it for just such
occasions. Use ½ level teaspoon
turmeric if saffron is hard to
obtain.

CASSEROLE OF PHEASANT

Serves 4

25g (1oz) butter
1 tablespoon oil
1 pheasant, plucked, drawn and
   jointed
175g (6oz) button onions, peeled
3 level tablespoons flour
400ml (¾ pint) chicken stock
1 wine glass red wine
bouquet garni
finely grated rind and juice of
   half an orange
salt and pepper
100g (4oz) button mushrooms,
   washed and sliced
1 dessertspoon redcurrant jelly
small triangles of fried bread to
   garnish
chopped parsley

1. Preheat oven to moderate,
180°C (350°F) or gas 4.
2. Heat butter and oil in a frying
pan and fry pheasant joints until
golden brown all over. Drain well
over pan and transfer to a
casserole.
3. Place onions in fat remaining
in the pan and fry until lightly
browned, then transfer with a
draining spoon to casserole.
4. Sprinkle flour into fat
remaining in the pan and stir over
gentle heat for 1 minute.
5. Remove pan from heat and
gradually blend in stock and
wine.
6. Return to heat, bring to the
boil and simmer for 2 minutes,
stirring continuously.
7. Add bouquet garni, orange rind
and juice and season well with
salt and pepper. Pour into
casserole.
8. Cover closely with lid or foil
and cook in centre of oven for
about 1 hour.
9. Stir in mushrooms and
redcurrant jelly and continue
cooking for a further 30 minutes,
or until pheasant is tender.
10. Garnish with triangles of fried
bread and sprinkle with parsley.
11. Serve with redcurrant jelly, if
liked.

*Serve colourful Valencia paella, △
the famous Spanish rice, seafood
and chicken dish, to remind
everyone of holidays.*

*Casserole of pheasant is cooked in ▷
red wine sauce with mushrooms.*

ROAST TURKEY

Serves 6

1 turkey (about 5 kilo or 10lb)
**500g (1lb) fresh chestnuts or 1
   can (275g or 10oz) whole
   chestnuts in water**
**225g (8oz) pie pork or veal,
   minced**
**175g (6oz) streaky bacon,
   minced**
salt and pepper
pinch of ground nutmeg
**500g/1lb streaky bacon, fairly
   thickly sliced**
500g (1lb) chipolata sausages
1 level tablespoon plain flour
**400ml (¾ pint) stock made from
   the giblets**
watercress to garnish

1. Preheat oven to moderately
hot, 200°C (400°F) or gas 6.
2. Weigh the bird and calculate
the cooking time by allowing 20
minutes to the 0.5 kilo (lb) plus an
extra 20 minutes.
3. If using fresh chestnuts, snip
the top of each chestnut with a
pair of scissors then place them in
a pan of water.
4. Bring the water to the boil and
boil the chestnuts for 2 minutes,
then remove them from the heat.
5. Remove the outer and inner
shells, keeping the chestnuts as
whole as possible and place them
in a mixing bowl. (Drain the
canned chestnuts.)
6. Add the minced pork or veal
and bacon with plenty of
seasoning and the ground nutmeg.
7. Bind the ingredients together
to form a stuffing.
8. Starting at the neck end work
the stuffing very carefully in
between the skin and the breast to
about halfway along the breast.
9. Do not split the skin if possible
or the stuffing will burst out
during cooking. Push the stuffing
under the breast skin, making
sure the shape of the bird is
retained. The stuffing helps to
keep the breast moist as well as
giving it a good flavour.
10. Tuck the loose skin which
covered the neck under the wings
to help keep the stuffing in place.
11. Put the turkey in a roasting
tin and cover it completely with
the rashers of streaky bacon
starting at the legs, then cover
the tin with foil.

12. Roast the bird in the centre of
the oven for 1 hour then reduce
the heat to moderate, 180°C
(350°F) or gas 4, for the rest of the
cooking time. If the bird is really
large, that is above 9 kilos or 18lb,
reduce the heat after the first
hour to cool, 150°C (300°F) or gas
2.
13. Baste the bird after the first
hour.
14. Half an hour before the end of
the cooking time remove the foil
and bacon so the skin can brown.
Place pricked sausages around
the turkey.
15. Transfer the cooked turkey to
a plate and surround with the
sausages. Leave in a warm place
while making the gravy.
16. Drain almost all the fat from
the tin leaving about 1
tablespoon.
17. Stir in the flour then
gradually blend in the stock.
18. Place the tin over the heat,
and stirring all the time, bring the
gravy to the boil.
19. Check it for seasoning before
pouring it into a gravy boat.
20. Serve the turkey garnished
with watercress.

PIQUANT TURKEY LEGS

Serves 4

4 turkey legs
salt and pepper
½ teaspoon cayenne pepper
1 teaspoon made mustard
40g (1½oz) butter

1. Skin the turkey legs and slit
them with a sharp knife.
2. Sprinkle with salt, pepper and
cayenne pepper.
3. Spread with mustard and leave
for 2 hours.
4. Grill for about 20–30 minutes
until golden, then top each leg
with a cutlet frill.
5. Serve on a bed of lettuce with
watercress and sliced tomatoes.
Accompany with slices of crusty
French bread.

△ *Always serve your Christmas
Roast turkey with a tasty stuffing
and all the trimmings.*

◁ *To flavour Piquant turkey legs, the
flesh is slashed, then spread with
mustard and grilled until golden.*

TURKEY TETRAZZINI

Serves 4–6

225g (8oz) spaghetti
1 celery stick, chopped
1 small onion, chopped
1 can mushrooms, thinly sliced
75g (3oz) butter
1 can (275g or 10oz) cream of
    chicken soup
150ml (¼ pint) milk
50g (2oz) sharp Cheddar cheese,
    grated
2 tablespoons sherry (optional)
salt and pepper
225g (8oz) turkey, cooked and
    diced
grated Parmesan cheese

1. Preheat oven to moderate,
180°C (350°F) or gas 4.
2. Cook spaghetti in boiling,
salted water till tender. Drain and
keep hot.
3. Cook celery, onion, and
mushrooms in butter till tender.
4. Add soup, milk, cheese and
sherry if used. Season well.
5. Cook over low heat till cheese
has melted. Add turkey and pour
over spaghetti.
6. Stir and place in casserole.
Sprinkle with Parmesan and bake
in centre of oven for 20–25
minutes.

===== COOK'S TIP =====

Another way to use up Christmas
turkey in a hot dish. Make a note of
the ingredients and add them to the
store cupboard well before the
Christmas rush begins. Turkey
tetrazzini would go well with a
green salad and garlic bread (see
next Cook's Tip).

TURKEY SALAD

Serves 4

4 tablespoons oil
1 teaspoon curry powder
salt and pepper
1 lemon
1 tablespoon chopped parsley
225g (8oz) cooked turkey, diced
1 can (275g or 10oz) potatoes,
    drained and sliced

1. Place oil, curry powder, salt,
pepper, grated rind of half a
lemon and juice from whole lemon
and parsley in a screw-topped jar.
Shake well till ingredients are
blended.
2. Mix together turkey and
potatoes.
3. Pour dressing over turkey
mixture. Toss well and leave,
covered, for 1 hour. Serve on
lettuce, garnish with tomato
slices and watercress.

===== COOK'S TIP =====

Garlic bread has a heavenly smell
and goes well with many dishes.
Slice a French bread loaf through
the middle. Spread butter on cut
sides of bread and sprinkle lightly
with garlic powder or garlic salt;
sandwich together, cover bread
with foil and bake in a moderately
hot oven 200°C (400°F) or gas 6, for
10 minutes. If the oven is not being
used, then place bread under the
grill. Warm gently to melt butter
and to soften the bread without
toasting it.

*Tempting Turkey tetrazzini is a △
cheese, mushroom and turkey
sauce served on spaghetti.*

*For a filling, spicy cold dish, try ▷
Turkey salad. Leftover vegetables
and hard-boiled eggs may be
added.*

ORANGE-SAUCED DUCK

Serves 4

1 oven-ready duckling
50g (2oz) flour, seasoned with
 salt and pepper
3 tablespoons olive oil
1 garlic clove
400ml (¾ pint) chicken stock
3 oranges, halved
pinch of mixed herbs
1 tablespoon Cognac (optional)
225g (8oz) long-grain rice,
 cooked
1 small packet frozen peas
watercress
few lettuce leaves
1 orange, peeled and cut into
 segments
10 glacé cherries, halved

1. Preheat oven to very moderate,
170°C (325°F) or gas 3.
2. Remove giblets, wash body and
dry thoroughly.
3. Joint duckling into 4 portions
and coat in seasoned flour.
4. Fry until browned in hot oil to
which crushed garlic has been
added.
5. Remove joints and drain well
on kitchen paper.
6. Add flour to oil and make roux.
Add stock and cook over a low
heat to make the sauce.
7. Add the orange juice, scraped
out orange pulp (from the 3
oranges), herbs and season well.
8. Place joints in an ovenware
dish, coat with sauce and bake in
centre of oven for about 1½ hours
or until tender.
9. Remove the duckling portions
from the sauce and add Cognac, if
used.
10. Place the portions on a bed of
cooked rice and peas, spoon a
little sauce over and serve the
remainder of the sauce separately.
11. Garnish with half orange
shells filled with sprigs of
watercress.
12. Accompany with an orange
salad, made with lettuce leaves,
orange segments and glacé
cherries.

===== COOK'S TIP =====

To make a roux, heat the oil or fat
in a pan, add the flour and cook
over low heat for 2 minutes.
Remove from heat and add all cold
stock at once, stir well and return
to high heat, stirring quickly until
boiling. Turn down heat and cook a
further 2 minutes before using.

△ *When making delicious Orange-
sauced duck, choose a young bird:
ducks mature rapidly.*

◁ *A dinner party dish to impress
your guests, Duckling with grapes
recipe comes from Madeira.*

DUCKLING WITH GRAPES

Serves 4

1 oven-ready duckling (about 2
 kilo or 4lb)
salt and pepper
500g (1lb) green grapes
 (seedless if possible)
½ bottle Madeira wine
50g (2oz) butter
sprigs of watercress
lettuce leaves
1 orange, peeled and cut into
 skinless segments
few glacé cherries, halved
few slices of cucumber

1. Sprinkle duckling with salt
and pepper. Prick skin with a
fork.
2. Keep seedless grapes whole or
cut large grapes in half and
remove pips.
3. Place duckling and grapes in a
bowl, pour Madeira wine over and
leave to marinate overnight.
4. Preheat oven to moderate,
180°C (350°F) or gas 4.
5. Stuff about half the grapes
inside the duckling together with
the butter, then place in a
casserole.
6. Pour half the wine into the
casserole and keep remaining
wine and grapes on one side.
7. Cook, uncovered, in centre of
oven for 1½ hours.
8. Drain off fat from dish and add
remaining wine. Return to oven
for a further 30 minutes, or until
duckling is tender.
9. Place duckling on a serving
dish and garnish with remaining
grapes and sprigs of watercress.
10. Surround with lettuce leaves,
orange segments, halved glacé
cherries and cucumber slices.
Serve the sauce separately.

Fish dishes

Fish is quick to cook and nutritious to eat. There are many types of fish available these days and varied ways in which to cook it, from speedy casseroles to fancy pies. Fish is not quite the budget food it used to be, but there are recipes included for canned fish as well as fresh and frozen. Buy fish that is very fresh and cook the same day if possible.

WESTSIDE HERRINGS

Serves 4

4 large herrings or other oily
 fish
1 tablespoon made mustard
1 tablespoon tomato purée
good pinch of marjoram
salt
freshly ground black pepper
2 tablespoons single cream
1 level teaspoon sugar
2 teaspoons finely grated onion
a little melted butter
150ml ($\frac{1}{4}$ pint) cider
150ml ($\frac{1}{4}$ pint) water
paprika pepper

1. Preheat oven to moderate,
180°C (350°F) or gas 4.
2. Remove herring heads with
scissors and discard.
3. Scrape each herring from tail
to head with back of knife to
remove scales. Slit fish along
underside to tail and remove roe
and blood vessels.
4. Open each fish out and place
cut side down on board. Press
firmly along centre backbone to
flatten fish.
5. Turn over and remove
backbone.
6. Trim tails and fins with
scissors, then rinse and pat dry on
kitchen paper.
7. Blend together mustard,
tomato purée, marjoram, salt,
pepper, cream, sugar and onion.
8. Spread prepared mixture over
herrings, roll up neatly and
arrange in a shallow casserole.
9. Brush tops with butter.
10. Pour mixture of cider and
water into dish.
11. Cover closely with lid or foil
and cook in centre of oven for
about 40 minutes, or until fish is
cooked through.
12. Allow to cool in dish then
drain well, sprinkle with a little
paprika pepper and serve with
salad.

HERRINGS WITH RED CABBAGE

Serves 4

25g (1oz) butter
2 medium onions, chopped
750g (1$\frac{1}{2}$lb) red cabbage, finely
 shredded
75g (3oz) soft brown sugar
4 tablespoons wine vinegar
salt and pepper
4 herrings or other oily fish

1. Preheat oven to moderate,
180°C (350°F) or gas 4.
2. Melt butter, add onion and fry
for about 5 minutes without
browning.
3. Add red cabbage and cook a
further 5 minutes.
4. Stir in sugar, vinegar, salt and
pepper. Transfer to casserole,
cover and bake in oven for 2
hours or till tender.
5. Clean herrings and place on
top of red cabbage for last 20
minutes of cooking time.

=== **COOK'S TIP** ===

We are used to red cabbage pickled
and used with dishes but here the
raw cabbage is prepared as part of
the dish. To grate finely, after
washing, cut the cabbage into
quarters and grate each quarter on
the cheese side of the grater. Leave
any really hard ribs and chop these
finely with a knife later. The
herrings can be cleaned and de-
headed if you prefer. Salt rubbed
inside the cavity will help remove
blood and black skin.

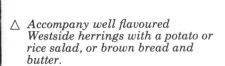

△ *Accompany well flavoured
Westside herrings with a potato or
rice salad, or brown bread and
butter.*

◁ *A hot, piquant dish, serve Herring
with red cabbage with baked jacket
potatoes.*

FRUITED HERRINGS

Serves 4

4 herrings or other oily fish
salt
Tabasco sauce
50g (2oz) butter, melted
paprika pepper
1 grapefruit
1 orange
2 tomatoes
watercress to garnish

1. Score fish with a knife, then place it on aluminium foil in grill pan.
2. Sprinkle with salt and Tabasco sauce. Pour half the fat over and sprinkle with paprika pepper.
3. Grill until fish is cooked, allowing 5–6 minutes on each side for whole fish.
4. Arrange fish on a hot serving dish, pour remaining fat over.
5. Garnish with half slices of grapefruit, orange and tomato and top with watercress sprigs.

=== **COOK'S TIP** ===

Tabasco sauce is a hot pepper sauce and should be treated with respect as a few drops add interest but too much can ruin a dish. The serving suggestion of salad and fruit with herring is good as herrings are oily fish rich in vitamin A and D. Be sure to hand French bread or rolls with fish to help take care of the little tickly bones.

BELL INN SMOKIES

Serves 4

4 smokies or baby haddock
  fillets
4 tomatoes
25g (1oz) butter
just under 250ml (½ pint) single
  cream
freshly ground black pepper
50g (2oz) Parmesan or Gruyère
  cheese, finely grated

1. Preheat oven to moderate, 180°C (350°F) or gas 4.
2. Trim tails and fins from fish, then strip off skin and remove bones and flake fish.
3. Skin tomatoes, cut in half and scoop out seeds with a teaspoon. Chop flesh roughly.
4. Grease four individual soufflé dishes 9cm (3½ inches) in diameter, with butter.
5. Pour 1 tablespoon cream into each dish, then add flaked fish and chopped tomatoes.
6. Sprinkle with pepper and pour remaining cream over. Cover with grated cheese.
7. Place dishes on a baking sheet and cook, uncovered, in centre of oven for about 20 minutes, or until cooked through.
8. Place under a hot grill to brown tops and serve immediately.

=== **COOK'S TIP** ===

To remove skin from a fish fillet (no bone), place fish on board, tail towards you. Take a French cook's knife and hold at right angles to the fish. Grasp the tail in the left hand and push the knife against the flesh, pushing forward rather than cutting flesh off the skin. Continue to push until head is reached.

For a snack with a difference, △ make Fruited herrings and serve with hot, crusty French bread.

Bell Inn smokies come from the ▷ famous Bell Inn at Aston Clinton in Buckinghamshire.

SCOTTISH SUPPER

Serves 2–3

1 can (397g or 14oz) sweetcorn
   kernels
500g (1lb) smoked, boneless cod
   or other white fish fillet
25g (1oz) butter
salt and pepper
150ml ($\frac{1}{4}$ pint) single cream
paprika pepper

1. Preheat oven to moderate,
180°C (350°F) or gas 4.
2. Drain sweetcorn. Skin fish if
necessary and cut into strips.
3. Arrange layers of sweetcorn
and fish in a casserole, dotting
with a little butter and seasoning
with salt and pepper between each
layer.
4. Pour cream over top.
5. Cook, uncovered, in centre of
oven for about 25–30 minutes, or
until fish is cooked through.
6. Sprinkle with paprika pepper
before serving.

=== **COOK'S TIP** ===

To remove skin from fish see Cook's
Tip for Bell Inn Smokies, page 69.
  Other smoked fish are haddock
and mackerel and these could be
used in this recipe. Serve with a
green salad and French bread or
cooked noodles.

FISH CURRY

Serves 4

1 large onion, chopped
50g (2oz) butter
3 tomatoes, skinned and
   quartered
750g (1$\frac{1}{2}$lb) cod or other white
   fish fillet
2 teaspoons curry powder
salt
pinch of sugar

1. Fry onion in butter and add the
tomatoes
2. Skin fish, cut into pieces and
coat with curry powder.
3. Fry fish until brown, then add
salt and sugar.
4. Cover and simmer for 10
minutes.
5. Serve with hot rice and
poppadoms.

=== **COOK'S TIP** ===

Poppadoms are an ideal
accompaniment to curries. They
are normally bought in cans and
you should allow one per person.
Fry one at a time in hot fat – it
will puff up during cooking. Keep
them warm in the oven.

△ *Add poached eggs to quick-to-
prepare Scottish supper for a more
substantial meal.*

◁ *Fish curry is the quickest curry to
make. Serve with a tomato,
cucumber and yogurt side dish.*

FISH LATTICE

Serves 4–5

shortcrust pastry made with
    225g (8oz) flour (see Basic
    recipes, page 7)
500g (1lb) cod or other white
    fish fillets, cooked and flaked
little canned pimento, chopped
cream to bind
salt and pepper
1 medium egg, beaten
paprika pepper to garnish

1. Preheat oven to moderately
hot, 220°C (400°F) or gas 6.
2. Use most of the pastry to line a
shallow baking or Swiss roll tin.
3. Mix the fish with the pimento
and cream.
4. Season carefully to taste.
5. Spoon into pastry-lined tin.
6. Cut rest of pastry into strips
and arrange, lattice style, over
the filling.
7. Brush pastry with egg.
8. Bake, in centre of preheated
oven, for 25 minutes.
9. Serve hot, garnished with a
little paprika pepper, if liked.

===== COOK'S TIP =====

You could use an alternative filling
of other white fish such as haddock
or coley in this dish. In place of
cream, use ½ can condensed cream
of mushroom soup. For an extra
special pie, add a small can of
shrimps (drained) to the white fish
filling. This pie could be served
cold with salad.

CRUNCHY COD CASSEROLE

Serves 4

500g (1lb) cod or other white
    fish fillet, or 1 packet (325g or
    13oz) frozen cod or white fish
    fillets
1 large onion, chopped
25g (1oz) butter
50g (2oz) button mushrooms,
    sliced
1 can (400g or 14oz) tomatoes or
    225g (8oz) fresh tomatoes,
    skinned and sliced
1 tablespoon chopped parsley
salt and pepper
4 slices bread, crusts removed
    and well buttered
25g (1oz) Cheddar cheese,
    grated

1. Preheat oven to moderate,
180°C (350°F) or gas 4.
2. Arrange cod in buttered,
shallow, ovenproof dish.
3. Fry onion in butter till soft.
Add mushrooms and fry another
minute.
4. Stir in tomatoes (drain juice
from canned tomatoes), parsley
and seasoning.
5. Pour over fish and bake,
covered in centre of oven for
about 40 minutes.
6. Cut slices of bread into
triangles and arrange on a baking
sheet close together.
7. Sprinkle with grated cheese
and bake in oven on shelf below
fish.
8. Arrange bread round the
outside of fish before serving.

*An attractive fish pie to tempt the △
family, serve Fish lattice either hot
or cold.*

*Crunchy cod casserole contains ▷
tomatoes, mushrooms and fish
surrounded with baked bread
triangles.*

COD WITH GRAPES

Serves 4

4 cod or other white fish cutlets
1 shallot, sliced
50g (2oz) button mushrooms,
sliced
600ml (1 pint) fish stock
a little white wine (optional)
salt and pepper
25g (1oz) butter
25g (1oz) flour
150ml (¼ pint) milk
100g (4oz) white grapes,
skinned and seeded
watercress to garnish

1. Preheat oven to moderately
hot, 190°C (375°F) or gas 5.
2. Wash the fish and put into a
baking dish.
3. Add the shallot and
mushrooms. Cover with stock and
the wine, if used.
4. Season, and bake on centre
shelf of oven for 20 minutes.
5. Reserve 150ml (¼ pint) of the
liquid. Discard onion; reserve
mushrooms and keep hot.
6. Arrange the fish on a dish.
7. To make a sauce, melt the
butter in a saucepan and add the
flour.
8. Remove from heat and
gradually stir in stock and the
milk.
9. Season and boil sauce, stirring,
until it thickens. Add most of the
grapes.
10. Pour sauce over the fish and
garnish with watercress, the rest
of the grapes and mushrooms.

COD PALERMO

Serves 6

6 frozen or fresh cod or other
white fish steaks
2 medium onions
1 tablespoon salad oil
225g (8oz) tomatoes
2 heaped tablespoons finely
chopped parsley
salt and pepper
2 tablespoons Marsala

1. Preheat oven to moderately
hot, 200°C (400°F) or gas 6.
2. Arrange fish in a buttered
ovenproof dish.
3. Chop onions finely and dry in
the oil until pale golden.
4. Skin and chop tomatoes and
add to pan of onions with all
remaining ingredients, except
Marsala.
5. Cover and simmer for 10
minutes.
6. Add Marsala. Spoon equal
amounts over fish steaks then
cook, uncovered, in centre of oven
for 20 minutes.
7. Serve with freshly boiled long-
grain rice or noodles.

=== **COOK'S TIP** ===

Chinese fine noodles are for soups
but the broader pasta Italian-type
noodles make a change from
potatoes or rice to use with many
other dishes. Add 1 teaspoon oil to
the cooking water and it will help
keep the noodles from sticking
together. It also helps to cook in
plenty of water. Noodles are one of
the quickest pastas, they are
cooked in approximately 7 minutes.
Drain well. To keep hot, grease dish
well, pour in noodles, add 2
tablespoons margarine, toss well
and cover. Keep over hot water or
in a cool oven.

△ *When serving Cod with grapes for
a special occasion, use half stock
and half white wine.*

◁ *Cod Palermo is a mouthwatering
Italian fish dish. Serve with an
Italian white wine and salad.*

FISH BOAT

Serves 4–6

puff pastry made with 225g
   (8oz) flour (see Basic recipes,
   page 7)
1 medium egg, beaten
25g (1oz) butter
25g (1oz) flour
300ml (½ pint) milk
2 cod steaks, cooked and flaked
1 heaped teaspoon made
   English mustard
175g (6oz) peeled prawns
4 whole prawns to garnish

1. Preheat oven to moderately
hot, 200°C (400°F) or gas 6.
2. Roll out the pastry fairly thinly
to make an oblong.
3. Cut off a 1cm (½ inch) wide
strip all the way round.
4. Brush the edges of the pastry
oblong with egg and put the strips
on to look like a picture frame.
Brush the strip with egg.
5. Put on a baking sheet and
bake, in centre of preheated oven,
for 20 minutes.
6. While the pastry is cooking,
melt the butter in a small pan.
Stir in the flour and cook gently
for 2 minutes, stirring.
7. Gradually whisk in the milk.
8. Bring to the boil, stirring until
thickened.
9. Stir in the flaked cod, mustard
and peeled prawns and heat
gently.
10. Put the fish mixture in the
cooked pastry boat.
11. Garnish each corner with a
whole prawn. Serve hot.

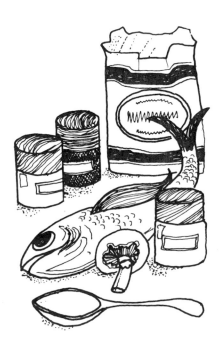

GRILLED HALIBUT WITH SPICED SAUCE

Serves 4

4 halibut, cod or other white
   fish steaks, about 175g (6oz)
   each
25g (1oz) plain flour, seasoned
   with salt and pepper
75g (3oz) butter
½ level teaspoon powdered basil
½ level teaspoon marjoram
pinch of mixed spice
¼ level teaspoon powdered
   mustard
1 level teaspoon tomato purée
2 tablespoons lemon juice
lemon slices to garnish

1. Wash and dry fish. Coat with
seasoned flour.
2. Melt 25g (1oz) butter in grill
pan or shallow ovenware dish and
lay fish in it.
3. Spoon a little butter over fish
and grill them under medium
heat. Add another 25g (1oz) butter
and increase heat a little. Grill till
golden on both sides.
4. Meanwhile, melt remaining
butter in pan and blend in herbs,
spice and mustard. Add tomato
purée, lemon juice and salt and
pepper to taste.
5. Spoon sauce over fish. Lower
grill heat and cook for 5 minutes.
6. Garnish with lemon slices and
serve.

══ COOK'S TIP ══

This dish can also be cooked in the
oven. Wash and prepare fish as in
steps 1 and 2 of recipe. Make the
sauce as step 4, using all the butter,
and pour over the fish. Cover with
foil. Bake in a moderately hot oven,
190°C (375°F) or gas 5, for 25
minutes. Remove cover and cook
for a further 5 minutes or until
browned. Garnish with lemon
slices.
   Adapting a recipe to cook in the
oven can save fuel if other dishes
are being cooked at the same time:
for example, baked jacket potatoes
and a pudding.

*A delightful cod and prawn △
mixture in a melt-in-the-mouth
pastry case, serve Fish boat for
any occasion.*

*Serve Grilled halibut with ▷
spiced sauce when the family are
tired of fried fish.*

MOCK PIZZA

Serves 4

shortcrust pastry made with
175g (6oz) flour (see Basic
recipes, page 7)
1 can (500g or 1lb) tomatoes
2 fresh haddock steaks, cooked
and flaked
salt and pepper
good pinch of thyme
knob of butter
3 slices processed cheese
few thin strips anchovy fillets
little olive or corn oil
few black olives to garnish

1. Preheat oven to moderately
hot, 200°C (400°F) or gas 6.
2. Roll out the pastry and use to
line a 18- or 20-cm (7- or 8-inch)
pie plate or sandwich tin.
3. Bake pastry blind (see page 7),
in centre of preheated oven, for 20
minutes.
4. Drain juice off tomatoes – the
juice is not needed.
5. Heat the tomatoes in a pan.
6. Meanwhile, in another pan,
heat the fish with seasoning,
thyme and a knob of butter.
7. Spoon fish mixture into the
pastry case.
8. Arrange the heated tomatoes
on half the flan.
9. Cover the other half of the flan
with cheese slices.
10. Arrange strips of anchovy on
top of the flan.
11. Brush the tomatoes with a
little oil and put under a hot
grill until cheese is melted and
golden.
12. Garnish with olives and
serve hot.

══ COOK'S TIP ══

A large can of tuna fish 200g (7oz)
could replace the haddock steaks
but drain off the oil before use. The
other ingredients you are likely to
have in the store cupboard, too, and
could be made quickly as a hot
supper for an unexpected visitor.

SPINACH AND FISH FLAN

Serves 4–5

shortcrust pastry made with
175g (6oz) flour (see Basic
recipes, page 7)
1 large packet frozen leaf
spinach, cooked
50g (2oz) button mushrooms,
sliced and stewed in lemon
juice
225g (8oz) smoked haddock,
cooked and flaked

1. Preheat oven to moderately
hot, 200°C (400°F) or gas 6.
2. Use the pastry to line a 18- or
20-cm (7- or 8-inch) flan ring or
sandwich tin and bake blind (see
page 7), in centre of preheated
oven, for 20 minutes, until golden.
3. Fill the cooked flan case with
hot chopped spinach, mushrooms
and haddock as illustrated.
4. Serve hot.

══ COOK'S TIP ══

Frozen spinach is such a help to the
housewife as it saves all the careful
preparation necessary with fresh
spinach. Cook as directed on the
packet. If in the last few minutes of
cooking the spinach seems to have
too much liquid, sprinkle in 2 level
teaspoons of flour, stir well and
cook a further 2 minutes. This will
prevent the pastry from becoming
soggy.

△ *Colourful and tasty Mock pizza is
made with a pastry base instead of
the traditional yeast dough base.*

◁ *For a change, use a mixture of
smoked and fresh fish in Spinach
and fish flan.*

SOLE MORNAY

Serves 4

2 Dover sole or flounder
juice of ½ lemon
300ml (½ pint) fish stock (make
    from fish bones and skin)
225g (8oz) hot, mashed potato
50g (2oz) butter
1 medium egg, beaten
25g (1oz) flour
100g (4oz) Cheddar cheese,
    grated
salt and pepper
sprigs of parsley
slices of lemon

1. Preheat oven to moderate,
180°C (350°F) or gas 4.
2. Wash, skin and fillet the sole.
3. Put the fillets in a buttered
ovenware dish, folding each in half.
4. Add the lemon juice and the
fish stock.
5. Cover the dish with foil or
buttered greaseproof paper.
6. Cook on centre shelf of oven
for 10 minutes.
7. Strain stock into a basin and
keep the fish hot.
8. Cream the potato with 25g
(1oz) butter and half the beaten
egg. Pipe it in rosettes round the
edge of a fireproof dish.
9. Brush potato gently with the
rest of the egg.
10. Heat the remaining butter,
add the flour and gradually beat
in the strained fish stock.
11. Cook until the sauce will coat
the back of a spoon. Stir in 75g
(3oz) cheese and season well with
salt and pepper.
12. Place the fish in the centre of
the piped potato.
13. Reheat the sauce and pour
over the sole.
14. Sprinkle with rest of cheese
and glaze lightly under the grill.
15. Garnish with parsley and
lemon slices and serve
immediately.

PENNY PIE

Serves 4

shortcrust pastry made with
    150g (5oz) flour (see Basic
    recipes, page 7)
1 medium egg, beaten
1 large can red salmon
¼ small cucumber
few radishes or tomato wedges
bottled mayonnaise to bind

1. Preheat oven to moderately
hot, 200°C (400°F) or gas 6.
2. Roll out the pastry and use
most of it to line a shallow 18-cm
(7-inch) pie plate.
3. From the rest of the pastry cut
out rounds the size of a 10p piece.
4. Wet these rounds and arrange
them, overlapping, all round the
edge of the pie.
5. Brush the pastry with egg
and bake blind (see page 7), in
centre of preheated oven, for 20
minutes, or until golden.
6. Leave pastry to cool.
7. Mix the salmon with the
chopped, unpeeled cucumber,
whole radishes or tomato
wedges and enough mayonnaise
to bind.
8. Spoon this mixture into
pastry case.
9. Serve cold with a green salad
and beetroot.

═══ COOK'S TIP ═══

This cold flan of salmon is best
prepared ahead of time, with the
filling chilled and added just before
serving. It is colourful with the red
salmon but drained tuna fish would
be an alternative. Quartered hard-
boiled eggs make a tasty garnish
with tuna.

For a dinner party to remember, △
serve delicate Sole mornay with
duchesse potatoes and green beans.

Penny pie is an unusual open, cold ▷
pie filled with delicious salmon
and cucumber. Serve in
summertime.

CREAMY KIPPER SCALLOPS

Serves 4

500g (1lb) kipper fillets
56g (2¼oz) butter
40g (1½oz) flour
400ml (¾ pint) milk
finely grated rind of 1 lemon
350g (12oz) potatoes
2 tablespoons milk

1. Cut kipper fillets into 1cm (½ inch) cubes and divide equally between four large scallop shells.
2. Melt 40g (1½oz) butter in a pan. Stir in flour and cook for 2–3 minutes without browning.
3. Remove from heat and gradually stir in milk. Bring to boil and cook for 3–4 minutes.
4. Stir in lemon rind. Divide sauce equally over kipper pieces.
5. Mash potatoes with remaining butter and the milk and pipe it round edge of shells.
6. Put under a hot grill just before serving.

=== **COOK'S TIP** ===

Other smoked fish could be used successfully in this and the next recipe. Try kippered or smoked mackerel but be sure to trim any head, fins etc. before use, as the fish is covered by a sauce.

KIPPER AND EGG KEDGEREE

Serves 4–6

2 packets frozen kipper fillets
50g (2oz) butter
175g (6oz) long-grain rice, boiled and well dried
3 hard-boiled eggs
salt and pepper
1 egg, beaten
4–5 tablespoons cream or milk
1 tablespoon prepared English mustard
parsley sprigs

1. Defrost kippers and reserve 2 fillets. Cut rest into big shreds.
2. Melt butter in a pan, add kipper pieces and shake over heat until hot.
3. Add rice and 2 eggs, coarsely chopped. Season to taste.
4. Shake over heat for a few minutes.
5. Beat egg, cream or milk and mustard together. Stir into kipper mixture in pan.
6. When hot, arrange in a serving dish and keep hot.
7. Grill remaining kipper fillets. Place on top of kedgeree.
8. Garnish with quarters of hard-boiled egg and sprigs of parsley.

△ *Dress up kippers and serve as Creamy kipper scallops for lunch or supper.*

◁ *For a more nutritious supper dish, make Kipper and egg kedgeree with brown rice.*

Vegetable dishes

More and more people are realizing that vegetables can be a meal in
themselves, not just a side dish. Carefully prepared, cooked and
attractively served, vegetables add colour and texture to meals, plus
valuable vitamins we all need. A wide variety of both our own seasonal
and other imported vegetables are available all year round, so try
serving small portions of two or three vegetables at a meal,
rather than one.

CAULIFLOWER CHEESE

Serves 4

1 cauliflower
50g (2oz) butter
50g (2oz) flour
600ml (1 pint) milk
salt and pepper
100g (4oz) cheese, grated
8 bacon rashers

1. Wash cauliflower and break into sprigs.
2. Put into a pan with a little salted, boiling water.
3. Cook for 10 minutes until tender.
4. Drain and put cauliflower in a pie dish.
5. Melt butter in a saucepan, mix in flour, beat in milk and season well.
6. Cook, stirring, until mixture thickens.
7. Add 65g (2½oz) cheese.
8. Pour sauce over the cauliflower and sprinkle with the rest of the cheese.
9. Grill until brown.
10. Roll up each bacon rasher and grill until crisp. Arrange round cauliflower and serve immediately.

=== **COOK'S TIP** ===

Cauliflower cheese is an old favourite. The recipe for cheese sauce could be used with other vegetables for a light but nourishing supper dish. Try cooked potatoes – put in layers in a greased ovenproof dish, covered with this sauce and browned in the oven. Combinations of peas, beans, courgettes, sweetcorn and broccoli all go well with cheese sauce.

CURRIED CAULIFLOWER

Serves 4

1 medium cauliflower
50–75g (2–3oz) butter
2 tomatoes, chopped
2 sticks celery, chopped
1 large onion, chopped
150ml (¼ pint) chicken or vegetable stock
1 dessertspoon curry powder
1 tablespoon chutney
2 hard-boiled eggs, chopped

1. Cut washed cauliflower into small sprigs. Blanch for 2 minutes in boiling, salted water and drain well.
2. Melt butter in a large frying pan. Toss cauliflower in this for a few minutes. Add tomato, celery and onion.
3. Mix together rest of ingredients, except the egg, and add to pan. Cover and simmer gently for 10 minutes.
4. Serve sprinkled with chopped hard-boiled egg.

=== **COOK'S TIP** ===

If you are looking for a dish to stretch your budget or for a vegetarian visitor, then try this curried cauliflower. It is nutritious and attractive to look at, with different coloured and shaped vegetables mixed together with hard-boiled eggs.

△ *Tasty Cauliflower cheese can be served by itself as a light supper dish or with bacon and sausages.*

◁ *Unusual Curried cauliflower makes an excellent accompaniment to ham and chicken.*

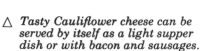

DANISH SWEET SOUR RED CABBAGE

Serves 4–6

1 medium red cabbage (about
  1.5 kilo or 3lb)
2 large cooking apples, peeled
50g (2oz) butter
100g (4oz) wine vinegar
1 tablespoon water
50g (2oz) granulated sugar
pinch of powdered cloves
salt and ground black pepper
2 large tablespoons redcurrant
  jelly

1. Shred the cabbage and grate
the apples.
2. Put them into a saucepan with
the butter.
3. Cook, covered, over gentle heat
until butter has melted.
4. Add the wine vinegar, water,
sugar and cloves; continue
cooking for 2 hours over gentle
heat.
5. Season with salt and pepper;
add the redcurrant jelly and cook
for a further 15 minutes.

CHEESE AND CABBAGE CASSEROLE

Serves 4

500g (1lb) white cabbage,
  shredded
300ml (½ pint) cheese sauce (see
  Basic recipes, page 6)
50g (2oz) cheese, grated

1. Cook cabbage in boiling, salted
water till just tender. Drain and
keep vegetable water for cheese
sauce, if liked.
2. Make cheese sauce, stir in
cooked cabbage and place in a
greased, ovenproof dish. Sprinkle
with cheese and brown under the
grill.

=== **COOK'S TIP** ===

Only one or two more steps makes
boiled cabbage into something
special. Shred the cabbage on the
slicing side of the grater and cook
in very little water until just
tender. Solid white cabbage shreds
well but if using green cabbage,
take a little extra time and a sharp
knife to cut evenly; it makes the
cabbage much more palatable.
Cheese sauce is a good way of using
up any oddments of cheese, as the
harder the cheese the easier it is to
grate.

*Danish sweet sour red cabbage can △
be prepared ahead and reheated. It
can also be served cold.*

*Serve quick-to-prepare Cheese and ▷
cabbage casserole with chops and
other grilled meats.*

AUBERGINES A LA PROVENCALE

Serves 4–6

3 medium aubergines
salt
4–5 tablespoons olive oil
500g (1lb) tomatoes, peeled and
  chopped
freshly ground black pepper
1 garlic clove, peeled and
  crushed
4 tablespoons fresh white
  breadcrumbs
1 tablespoon chopped parsley
25g (1oz) butter

1. Wash aubergines, trim off both
ends and cut into slices. Place in a
colander and sprinkle with salt.
Press down with a plate and leave
to stand for 1 hour so that the
excess moisture drains off.
2. Wash in cold water and dry on
kitchen paper.
3. Preheat oven to moderate,
180°C (350°F) or gas 4.
4. Heat oil in a frying pan and fry
aubergine slices until golden
brown on both sides. Drain.
5. Fry tomatoes in oil remaining
in the pan, or add a little more if
necessary, and season well with
salt and pepper. Add garlic.
6. Transfer to a shallow
casserole.
7. Overlap aubergine slices on top
of tomato mixture in casserole.
8. Mix breadcrumbs with parsley
and sprinkle over top of dish. Dot
with butter.
9. Cook, uncovered, in centre of
oven for about 30 minutes, or
until top is crisp and brown.

=== **COOK'S TIP** ===

Usually cheapest in the summer,
aubergine (egg plant) is a vegetable
new to some people but is not
difficult to prepare. Inside the
lovely purple skin, it has a spongy
flesh rather like a dryish marrow
and when cooked the flavour is
delicate but distinctive. The skin is
not always eaten but is left on in
some recipes for appearance. Make
sure fat or oil is hot enough when
frying or the aubergine will absorb
large quantities. When cooked, the
flesh turns to a clear grey green and
the small seeds are visible
throughout.

LOMBARDY CASSEROLE

Serves 4–6

2 medium aubergines
salt
2–3 tablespoons olive oil
225g (8oz) quick-cooking
  macaroni
15g (½oz) butter
1 can (265g or 9oz) tomato
  sauce or tomatoes
50g (2oz) Cheddar cheese, finely
  grated
50g (2oz) fresh breadcrumbs

1. Wash aubergines, trim off both
ends and cut into slices. Place in a
colander and sprinkle with salt.
Press down with a plate and leave
to stand for 1 hour, so that the
excess moisture drains off.
2. Wash in cold water and dry on
kitchen paper.
3. Preheat oven to moderate,
180°C (350°F) or gas 4.
4. Heat oil in a frying pan and fry
aubergine slices until golden
brown on both sides.
5. Cook macaroni in boiling,
salted water according to packet
directions, until just tender. Drain
well.
6. Grease a casserole with butter,
then fill with layers of fried
aubergines, macaroni and tomato,
finishing off with a layer of
tomato.
7. Sprinkle top with cheese and
breadcrumbs, then cook,
uncovered, above centre of oven
for 15–20 minutes, or until heated
through.

△ *Serve Aubergines á la Provençale
with French bread as a light lunch
or as a vegetable accompaniment.*

◁ *Lombardy casserole is a mixture of
aubergines, macaroni and tomatoes
with a crispy cheese and crumb
topping.*

RICE-STUFFED GREEN PEPPERS

Serves 4

4 medium green peppers
25g (1oz) butter
1 small onion, finely chopped
100g (4oz) minced beef
1 teaspoon chopped parsley
1 can (225g or 8oz) tomatoes
1 medium egg
50g (2oz) long-grain rice, boiled
salt and pepper

1. Preheat oven to moderate, 180°C (350°F) or gas 4.
2. Cut peppers in half and scoop out seeds.
3. Plunge them into boiling water for 5 minutes. Drain them and arrange in a buttered baking dish.
4. To prepare the stuffing, melt the butter and fry onion gently until tender.
5. Add minced beef and cook until brown.
6. Take pan off heat and stir in parsley, tomatoes and egg.
7. Add rice, season well and spoon filling into pepper shells.
8. Place in a greased ovenproof dish and bake in centre of oven for 45 minutes. Serve with tomato sauce.

=== **COOK'S TIP** ===

Take great care to remove all the seeds as these can be very hot, though the peppers are the sweet variety. Cooked chicken, corned beef or any cold leftover meat could be used in place of minced beef. Chop small or mince and add to the mixture.

JELLIED TOMATOES

Serves 4

25g (1oz) gelatine
300ml (½ pint) stock
4 large tomatoes
1 cooked carrot, diced
75g (3oz) cooked veal or chicken, shredded

1. Dissolve gelatine in stock over heat.
2. Cut tomatoes in half, scoop out pulp and sieve into stock. Add carrot and meat.
3. When jelly is nearly set, chill and spoon into tomato shells.
4. Leave to set firmly and serve with a green salad.

=== **COOK'S TIP** ===

These are most attractive for individual servings at a buffet or party supper. You can use a stock cube, but if you are using fresh stock be sure to remove all fat from the top. To do this either chill in the refrigerator for an hour or so for the fat to congeal and be lifted off. Alternatively, if the stock is warm, tear pieces of paper towel into 5cm (2 inch) strips and carefully draw across the top surface of the stock. The fat will stick to the paper and can be thrown away.

For a more substantial main △ course, double the amount of minced beef in Rice-stuffed green peppers.

Serve attractive Jellied tomatoes as ▷ a starter or as part of a buffet spread.

SUCCOTASH

Serves 6

1 medium can baked beans
1 medium can garden peas,
   strained
1 medium can corn kernels
225g (8oz) tomatoes, skinned
   and quartered
few drops Worcestershire
   sauce
1½ level teaspoons prepared
   mustard
salt and pepper

1. Place all the ingredients in a
large saucepan.
2. Heat through gently for 5
minutes.
3. Serve at once with sausages or
hamburgers.

=== **COOK'S TIP** ===

While this is primarily a vegetable
dish, the illustration shows the
succotash made into a main meal
by adding cut up sausages or
frankfurters. To make it more
substantial, add 100g (4oz) long
grain rice, cooked. The dish can be
heated in the oven in a flameproof
casserole at 190°C (375°F) or gas 5
for 30 minutes with the lid on.

BANANA TOGO

Serves 4–6

25g (1oz) butter
6 bananas, peeled and sliced
1 onion, peeled and finely
   chopped
2 tomatoes, peeled and chopped
pinch of turmeric powder

1. Preheat oven to moderate,
180°C (350°F) or gas 4.
2. Melt butter in a flameproof
casserole and add prepared
ingredients. Stir over gentle heat
for 1 minute.
3. Cover closely with lid or foil
and cook in centre of oven for
about 30 minutes, or until
bananas are cooked through.

△ *A very quick-to-prepare vegetable
dish, Succotash can be prepared
almost entirely from store cupboard
ingredients.*

◁ *Bananas cooked in onion and
tomato make Banana togo a good
accompaniment to ham and
sausages.*

GARDENERS' CASSEROLE

Serves 4–6

750g (1½lb) fresh French beans
1 bayleaf
pinch of nutmeg
25g (1oz) butter
15g (½oz) flour
300ml (½ pint) milk
½ level teaspoon mustard
100g (4oz) Cheddar cheese,
    grated
salt and pepper
1 tablespoon of cream or top of
    the milk

1. Preheat oven to hot, 220°C
(425°F) or gas 7.
2. Trim tops and tails from beans
and string if necessary. Leave
whole and cook in boiling, salted
water with bayleaf for 5–10
minutes, or until almost tender.
3. Drain well and discard bayleaf,
then toss in nutmeg and 15g (½oz)
butter.
4. Arrange beans in casserole and
keep warm.
5. Melt remaining butter in a
saucepan, sprinkle in flour and
stir over gentle heat for 2
minutes.
6. Remove pan from heat and
gradually blend in milk.
7. Return to heat, bring to the
boil and simmer for 2 minutes,
stirring continuously.
8. Remove pan from heat and beat
in mustard and 75g (3oz) cheese
until well blended. Season.
9. Stir cream or top of the milk
into hot cheese sauce and pour
over top of beans. Sprinkle top
with remaining cheese.
10. Cook, uncovered, towards top
of oven for about 15 minutes, or
until heated through and golden
brown.

POTATO PUFFS

Makes 12

choux pastry made with 35g (1¼
    oz) flour (see Basic recipes,
    page 7)
225g (8oz) mashed potato,
    creamed and sieved
50g (2oz) Cheddar cheese,
    grated

1. Preheat oven to moderate,
180°C (350°F) or gas 4.
2. Mix in the pastry with the
potato. Beat in cheese.
3. Put in a piping bag and pipe in
lengths, just like choux éclairs, on
a baking sheet.
4. Bake, in the centre of the
preheated oven, for 10–15
minutes, or until golden.
5. Serve hot.

=== COOK'S TIP ===

Choux pastry mixture is like a very
thick sauce, not like a true pastry
at all, so it is easy to blend in the
mashed potato and cheese. Serve
the puffs as savoury or cocktail
nibbles and have ready a thick
sauce or dip to serve with them. Try
tomato, curry or anchovy and
cream cheese.

*An exciting way to serve French △
beans is to cook them in the oven in
a cheese sauce as in Gardeners'
casserole.*

*Serve choux pastry Potato puffs ▷
with a dip at a cocktail party or as
an unusual starter.*

BEAN SOUFFLETTE

Serves 4

cheese pastry made with 100g
  (4oz) flour (see Basic recipes,
  page 7)
15g (½oz) lard
4 streaky bacon rashers,
  chopped
1 medium onion, chopped
1 can (500g or 1lb) baked beans
2 eggs, separated
1 dessertspoon mayonnaise
salt and pepper
1 tablespoon finely grated
  Parmesan cheese

1. Preheat oven to moderately
hot, 200°C (400°F) or gas 6.
2. Line a 20cm (8 inch) flan ring
with pastry and bake blind for
10–15 minutes.
3. Lower oven setting to
moderate, 180°C (350°F) or gas 4.
4. Melt lard in a pan. Fry bacon
and onion. Place in flan with
baked beans.
5. Blend egg yolks with
mayonnaise and seasoning. Whisk
egg whites till stiff. Fold into egg
yolk mixture.
6. Pile baked beans on top of
bacon and onion in the flan case.
Top with the egg mixture and
sprinkle with cheese. Bake in
centre of oven for 25–30 minutes
till firm and golden.

BEAN AND POTATO OPEN PIE

Serves 4–6

40g (1½oz) butter
1 kilo (2lb) potatoes
a little milk
salt and pepper
6g (¼oz) lard
1 medium onion, chopped
225g (8oz) minced beef
50g (2oz) mushrooms, sliced
1 can (500g or 16oz) baked
  beans
50g (2oz) cheese, grated

1. Preheat oven to very moderate,
170°C (325°F) or gas 3.
2. Grease a 20cm (8 inch) pie
plate with 20g (¾oz) butter.
3. Cook potatoes in salted water
till tender. Drain. Mash and
cream with rest of butter and a
little hot milk.
4. Season. Line pie plate with
potato and bake in centre of oven
for 15–20 minutes.
5. Melt lard in a pan and fry
onion till soft. Add meat and
mushrooms and cook for a further
10 minutes. Fold in baked beans.
6. Pile mixture into pie plate,
sprinkle with cheese and bake for
a further 30 minutes till potato is
crisp.

=== **COOK'S TIP** ===

Baked beans are a favourite in most
families but this is a way to dress
them up. The pie 'crust' is made
from mashed potato and this will
hold its shape better if 1 medium
egg, beaten, is added or very little
milk. For a meatless dish, leave out
the beef and add 50g (2oz) more
mushrooms.

△ *Tasty Bean Soufflette is a delicious
savoury flan to serve for supper.
Very popular with children.*

◁ *The 'pastry' case for Bean and
potato open pie is made from
mashed potatoes, saving pastry-
making time.*

Supper dishes

Suppers need to be quick to prepare, easy to serve and nutritious. If they can be eaten just with a fork, so much the better. Most of these dishes, which include a high proportion of eggs and cheese, can be prepared earlier in the day, ready to cook or reheat at suppertime. This suits many people who plan a supper in front of the fire or while watching television.

MACARONI CHEESE

Serves 6

25g (1oz) margarine
225g (8oz) onions, peeled and
    sliced
1 can 225g (8oz) tomatoes
75g (3oz) short cut macaroni

Sauce:
40g (1½oz) margarine
40g (1½oz) plain flour
400ml (¾ pint) milk
150ml (¼ pint) macaroni liquid
    (see method)
175g (6oz) Cheddar cheese,
    grated
1 level teaspoon made English
    mustard
salt and cayenne pepper

Topping:
50g (2oz) Cheddar cheese,
    grated
50g (2oz) fresh white
    breadcrumbs
100g (4oz) tomatoes, sliced
100g (4oz) streaky bacon
    rashers, de-rinded
15g (½oz) butter, melted

1. Preheat oven to moderately
hot, 190°C (375°F) or gas 5.
2. Melt the margarine in a pan,
add the onions and cook gently
until tender then stir in the
tomatoes and turn the mixture
into a greased ovenproof dish.
3. Cook the macaroni in boiling,
salted water for about 15 minutes,
or until a piece feels tender.
4. Drain it, reserving 150ml
(¼ pint) liquid for the sauce.
5. Melt the margarine in a pan
and stir in the flour.
6. Gradually blend in the cold
milk then stir in the macaroni
liquid.
7. Return the pan to the heat and
stirring all the time, bring to the
boil.
8. Simmer for a few minutes to
thicken.
9. Take the pan off the heat and
stir in the grated cheese, with the
mustard, salt and cayenne pepper
to season.
10. Stir in the macaroni then turn
it into the dish on top of the
tomato and onion mixture.
11. Mix the grated cheese and
breadcrumbs together for the top
and sprinkle them thickly over
the macaroni mixture.

12. Arrange the tomato slices and
bacon rashers on the surface of
the macaroni cheese and brush
the tomato slices with the melted
margarine.
13. Cook in the centre of the oven
for 40–45 minutes until the
surface is golden brown and
bubbling.

FRYPAN CASSEROLE

Serves 6

100g (4oz) onion, chopped
50g (2oz) fat
2 cans (400g or 14oz each)
    tomatoes
1 can (275g or 10 oz) mushrooms
1½ teaspoons salt
shake of pepper
¼ teaspoon basil
1 teaspoon Worcestershire
    sauce
225g (8oz) macaroni shells
1 can (350g or 12oz) luncheon
    meat, cut in thin strips
2 tablespoons chopped parsley

1. Fry onion in fat for about 5
minutes.
2. Add tomatoes, liquid from
mushrooms and seasonings. Bring
to boil.
3. Add macaroni, cover and
simmer for 10–15 minutes or until
tender.
4. Stir in meat and mushrooms.
Cover and reheat. Sprinkle
parsley on top and serve.

=== COOK'S TIP ===

A useful dish for camping or one
burner cooking. Most of the
ingredients are canned and would
travel well. If you have not brought
Worcestershire sauce, you can use
ketchup.
    Sausages or frankfurters would
go equally well and so would
meatballs.

△ *Rich, creamy Macaroni cheese
makes the perfect supper dish,
served with a salad.*

◁ *Frypan casserole is quick and easy
to prepare, and filling, too. Other
pasta shapes may be used.*

SPAGHETTI SUPPER DISH

Serves 6

50g (2oz) fresh breadcrumbs
2 medium eggs
500g (1lb) pork sausages or
    sausagemeat
1 medium onion, chopped
1 garlic clove, crushed or finely
    chopped (optional)
salt and pepper
1 can (425g or 15¾oz) spaghetti
    with tomato and cheese
    sauce
50g (2oz) cheese, grated

1. Preheat oven to moderately
hot, 200°C (400°F) or gas 6.
2. Mix breadcrumbs soaked in
half 1 beaten egg with sausages or
sausagemeat, onion, garlic and
seasoning.
3. Line a greased, 20-cm (8-inch)
flan ring with the mixture. Brush
with a little beaten egg and cook
in centre of oven for 20 minutes.
4. Lower oven setting to
moderate, 180°C (350°F) or gas 4.
5. Turn spaghetti into a pan and
heat gently. Strain off the sauce
and mix it with remaining beaten
egg.
6. Add spaghetti to sauce and
pour into the sausagemeat case.
Cook for a further 20 minutes in
centre of oven.
7. Sprinkle top with cheese and
grill till golden brown.

SPAGHETTI RAREBIT

Serves 4

75g (3oz) spaghetti
25g (1oz) butter
150ml (¼ pint) beer
pinch paprika pepper
pinch cayenne pepper
¼ teaspoon dry mustard
1½ teaspoons piquant table
    sauce or ketchup
225g (8oz) cheese, grated
4 slices bread, toasted

1. Cook the spaghetti in boiling
salted water for 15 minutes, until
just tender.
2. Drain and toss in the butter.
3. Place in a hot serving dish and
keep warm.
4. Pour the beer into a pan, add
the seasonings and heat gently.
5. When hot, add the cheese and
stir until melted.
6. Pour over the spaghetti.
7. Place spaghetti on toast, then
grill until cheese browns slightly.

═══ COOK'S TIP ═══

The beer is optional and 150ml
(¼ pint) of milk could be substituted,
if more to your family's taste. Any
dish using toast should be cooked
immediately before serving or the
toast will be soft and soggy.
However, it is possible to make the
spaghetti mixture and keep it
separate until the last minute.

Serve golden Spaghetti supper dish △
with baked tomatoes, cooked in the
oven at the same time.

Similar to Welsh rarebit, ▷
satisfying Spaghetti rarebit makes
a tasty alternative.

ITALIAN HAM AND PASTA SHELLS

Serves 4

25g (1oz) butter
1 onion, chopped
25g (1oz) flour
1 can (400g or 14oz) tomatoes
2 tablespoons tomato purée
150ml (¼ pint) chicken stock
salt and pepper
pinch of sugar
bouquet garni
1 tablespoon chopped parsley
1 can (300g or 11oz) ham, diced
175g (6oz) pasta shells, cooked
  quickly in boiling salted
  water

1. Melt the butter and fry the onion lightly.
2. Stir in the flour, add all the remaining ingredients apart from the pasta.
3. Bring to the boil, stirring all the time, and simmer for a further 5 minutes.
4. Remove the bouquet garni, adjust the seasoning and serve on the drained pasta shells.

COOK'S TIP

Canned ham could be replaced with fresh ham but it needs to be chunky. Try ham or picnic ham steaks cooked as directed on the package and then diced. Allow half a steak per person for an average serving.

LASAGNE WITH YOGURT TOPPING

Serves 4

Meat sauce:
15g (½oz) lard
1 medium onion, chopped
500g (1lb) lean minced beef
1 level teaspoon dried mixed
  herbs
1 can (425g or 15oz) peeled
  tomatoes
2 level teaspoons cornflour
1 tablespoon Worcestershire
  sauce

Cheese sauce:
25g (1oz) butter
25g (1oz) flour
300ml (½ pint) milk
¼ level teaspoon dry mustard
40g (1½oz) Cheddar cheese,
  grated
salt and pepper
6 sheets lasagne (100g or about
  4oz)

Yogurt topping:
1 carton (150ml or ¼ pint)
  natural yogurt
1 egg
15g (½oz) flour
1 tablespoon grated Parmesan
  cheese (optional)

1. Preheat oven to moderately hot, 190°C (375°F) or gas 5.
2. To make the sauce, melt lard in pan and gently fry onion for 3 minutes, until soft.
3. Add beef, herbs and tomatoes and bring to the boil, stirring.
4. Simmer, uncovered for 30 minutes.
5. Mix cornflour with Worcestershire sauce and stir into the meat.
6. Return to boil for 1 minute, stirring.
7. To make cheese sauce, melt butter in a pan, stir in flour off the heat and blend in milk. Return to heat and bring to boil, stirring.
8. Remove from heat. Add mustard, cheese and seasoning.
9. Cook the pasta according to the directions or place in boiling salted water for 11 minutes; drain.
10. To make up the dish, arrange the meat, lasagne and cheese sauce in layers, in an approximately 1.75 litre (3 pint) ovenproof dish, finishing with a layer of lasagne.
11. To make topping, combine yogurt, egg and flour, mix well and spoon over lasagne. Bake in the centre of the oven for 20–25 minutes, until topping is set.
12. If liked, sprinkle with grated Parmesan cheese and brown under hot grill.

△ *Cooked, diced chicken could be used instead of ham in tempting Italian ham and pasta shells.*

◁ *Mouthwatering Italian Lasagne with yogurt topping takes time to prepare but is well worth the effort.*

CHEESE AND CIDER FONDUE

Serves 4

1¼ level tablespoons cornflour
1½ tablespoons water
1 garlic clove
150ml (¼ pint) dry cider
225g (8oz) Cheddar cheese, grated
¾ level teaspoon vegetable extract
1 French loaf, cut into bite-sized cubes

1. Mix cornflour with water to a smooth cream.
2. Rub the inside of a heavy, flameproof casserole or fondue pan with cut garlic clove. Pour in the cider and put on medium heat.
3. Just before cider comes to the boil add cheese, a handful at a time. Stir well till cheese melts.
4. Add cornflour cream and vegetable extract. Continue to heat slowly, stirring all the time, until fondue thickens enough to coat back of a spoon.
5. Serve on hot plate or candle-warmers with cubed bread. Use fondue forks to spear bread cubes and dip them in the cheese.

═══ COOK'S TIP ═══

Fondue is fun for the whole family and not difficult to prepare. In order not to overcook the cheese and make it stringy, care should be taken not to overheat. To keep warm while dipping, the mixture could be put in the top of a double boiler or bowl placed over a pan of hot water. Table forks do just as well as fondue forks but do not make the bread pieces too large for small mouths.

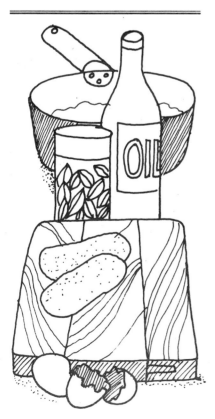

COUNTRY OMELETTE

Serves 2

1 small potato, cooked
1 small onion
2 tomatoes
2 tablespoons olive oil
shake of cayenne pepper
1 tablespoon tarragon vinegar
3 medium eggs
3 teaspoons water
salt and pepper

1. Peel and slice the potato. Skin and slice the onion and tomatoes.
2. Cook slowly in half the oil until tender but not browned.
3. Season with cayenne pepper and tarragon vinegar. Heat through well.
4. Beat the eggs lightly in a bowl, add the water and season well.
5. Add the potato mixture. Heat the remaining oil in a 23cm (9 inch) omelette pan. Pour in the egg mixture and cook, shaking the pan every so often.
6. Turn the omelette over when it is brown on one side.
7. Serve immediately, cut in half.

═══ COOK'S TIP ═══

Make your own tarragon vinegar with 1 tablespoon wine vinegar and a large pinch of tarragon. Use other herbs, such as oregano, basil and marjoram, for a change of flavour.

For an inexpensive party dish, △ choose cheese and cider fondue. Toasted wholemeal bread cubes and pineapple cubes are also good to dip.

Leftover mixed vegetables may be ▷ added to tasty Country omelette.

SUNRISE SAUSAGES

Makes 8

8 slices white bread
25g (1oz) lard or dripping
1 kilo (2lb) pork sausages
25g (1oz) butter or margarine
4 tablespoons milk
6 medium eggs
salt and pepper
2 tomatoes
watercress to garnish

1. Preheat oven to moderately hot, 190°C (375°F) or gas 5.
2. Cut the largest circle possible from each slice of bread.
3. Spread the lard or dripping over the slices then place them, fat side down, in a roasting tin.
4. Cut the sausages into pairs.
5. Along one side only of each pair make slits in the skin about 2.5cm (1 inch) apart and 1cm ($\frac{1}{2}$ inch) deep.
6. Curve the sausages into a circle with the slits on the outer side and lace each ring on to a circle of bread.
7. Bake the sausage circles in the centre of the oven for 40–45 minutes, until they are golden brown.
8. Meanwhile, melt the butter or margarine and add the milk.
9. Beat the eggs together, add them to the pan with the salt and pepper.
10. Scramble the eggs over a low heat.
11. When the sausage circles are cooked, transfer them to a serving dish.
12. Divide the scrambled egg between the sausages, placing it in the hole in the centre.
13. Top the egg with a slice of tomato and garnish with watercress sprigs.

EGG SCRAMBLE

Serves 2

225g (8oz) cooked chipolata
  sausages
50g (2oz) butter
2 thick rounds of bread
1 large eating apple
4 medium eggs
salt and pepper
2 tablespoons single cream or
  milk

1. Slice sausages and put into a saucepan with 25g (1oz) butter.
2. Spread remaining butter over the bread. Toast under a heated grill and keep hot.
3. Peel, core and chop the apple, add to sausages and heat through.
4. Beat eggs well with seasoning and cream or milk.
5. Pour into the pan and stir until just scrambled.
6. Pile eggs on to toast and serve hot with baked beans and green salad.

=== **COOK'S TIP** ===

Chipolata sausages come in cans if you cannot find fresh. Why not try some of the herb or spicy flavoured sausages? They would go well with the tartness of the apple.

△ *Sunrise sausages are an attractive new way of presenting scrambled egg and sausages.*

◁ *This special Egg scramble includes apple and sausages; a quick meal for a hungry family.*

POTATO SURPRISES

Serves 4

4 large potatoes
1 teaspoon salt
4 pork sausages
4 streaky bacon rashers
40g (1½oz) butter
25g (1oz) cheese, grated
salt and pepper
1 tablespoon cream

1. Preheat oven to moderately hot, 200°C (400°F) or gas 6.
2. Scrub the potatoes, rub with salt, prick and bake in centre of oven for 45 minutes.
3. Twist the sausages into small pieces. Prick and bake in the oven with the potatoes for 20 minutes.
4. Chop bacon rashers and fry till crisp.
5. Cut potatoes in half lengthways and scoop out most of the centre.
6. Brush with a little melted butter. Add cheese and season well.
7. Fill potatoes with the pieces of sausages and bacon.
8. Serve on a hot dish surrounded with the rest of the potatoes mashed with remaining butter and the cream.
9. Garnish with tomato quarters and sprigs of watercress.

SAUSAGE CAPERS

Serves 4

225g (8oz) onions, peeled and thinly sliced
4 large tomatoes, peeled and sliced
1 rounded tablespoon capers
salt
freshly ground black pepper
300ml (½ pint) chicken stock
500g (1lb) pork sausages

1. Preheat oven to moderately hot, 190°C (375°F) or gas 5.
2. Arrange onions in the base of a shallow casserole.
3. Cover with tomatoes.
4. Sprinkle capers over top and season with salt and pepper. Add stock.
5. Arrange sausages on top, cover closely with lid or foil and cook in centre of oven for about 30–40 minutes, or until onions are tender.
6. Remove lid and continue cooking for a further 10–15 minutes to brown sausages.

===== COOK'S TIP =====

Capers are bought in small jars and a little goes a long way. Small and green, not unlike a very small olive to look at, they are usually in vinegar. One tablespoon added to a sauce gives a distinctive, slightly hot taste.

Potato surprises are baked potatoes with sausages and cheese hidden inside them. △

Serve Sausage capers with mashed potatoes to mop up the delicious sauce. ▷

STUFFED CABBAGE LEAVES

Serves 6

6 large white cabbage leaves
500g (1lb) sausagemeat
1 large cooking apple, peeled,
cored and chopped
1 onion, finely chopped
grated rind of ½ lemon
1 teaspoon powdered sage
salt and pepper
1 can mulligatawny soup

1. Preheat oven to moderately hot, 190°C (375°F) or gas 5.
2. Blanch cabbage leaves for 2–3 minutes in boiling water. Drain and dry carefully. Remove the thick stem.
3. Mix sausagement, apple, onion, lemon rind, sage and seasoning. Divide into six portions, enclose each in a cabbage leaf and secure with cocktail sticks.
4. Place in shallow casserole. Pour the soup over the cabbage and bake in centre of oven for 35–40 minutes.

=== **COOK'S TIP** ===

Mulligatawny soup has a mild curry flavour. If you want a substitute then use tomato or oxtail soups. If condensed soup, dilute with water not milk. Other stuffings could be any cooked leftover meat or 100g (4oz) long grain rice, boiled.

SAUSAGEMEAT ROLL

Serves 5

suet crust pastry made with
350g (12oz) flour (see Basic
recipes, page 7)
1 medium egg, beaten
500g (1lb) pork sausagemeat
3 medium hard-boiled eggs,
shelled

1. Preheat oven to moderately hot, 190°C (375°F) or gas 5.
2. Roll out pastry to a neat oblong. Wet edges with egg.
3. Form the sausagemeat into a thin oblong.
4. Put the eggs, a little apart, lengthwise down centre of oblong.
5. Fold sausagemeat over eggs to make a roll shape.
6. Put this roll in the centre of the pastry and fold over all the edges. Seal with your fingers.
7. Put on a greased baking sheet. Brush with beaten egg.
8. Bake, in centre of preheated oven, for 40–45 minutes, or until golden.
9. Serve hot.

=== **COOK'S TIP** ===

This recipe takes a little time to prepare but is worth all the trouble. When forming the sausagemeat, flour both your hands and the meat and this will help to prevent sticking. Be sure to pinch the pastry together well as the filling may burst out. Sausage meat roll should be served hot but allow it to rest in a warm place for 5 minutes before serving as this will make it easier to slice.

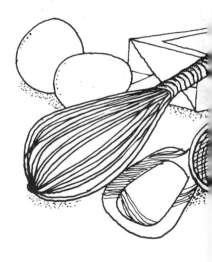

△ *Stuffed cabbage leaves provide a hearty supper dish. Serve with rice or boiled potatoes.*

◁ *A filling yet economical dish, Sausagemeat roll is made using light and spongy suet crust pastry.*

BACON AND BEEF ROLL

Serves 4

225g (8oz) lean raw minced beef
1 heaped tablespoon finely
    chopped parsley
4 firm tomatoes, chopped
2 salad onions, finely chopped
salt and black pepper
225g (8oz) back bacon, chopped
25g (1oz) oatmeal
1 teaspoon made mustard
1 egg

1. Preheat oven to moderately
hot, 200°C (400°F) or gas 6.
2. Mix all ingredients well
together and shape into a neat
roll.
3. Wrap in foil and bake in centre
of oven for 1½ hours.
4. Serve hot or cold on lettuce,
garnished with cucumber slices
and pineapple pieces.

FARMHOUSE SUPPER DISH

Serves 4

3 medium onions
3 sharp eating apples or 1
    cooking apple
4 bacon rashers
75g (3oz) butter
salt and pepper
4 medium eggs

1. Slice onions and unpeeled
apples.
2. Cut up bacon.
3. Heat butter in a large frying
pan, and add onion, apple, bacon
and seasoning.
4. Cook until onions are tender.
5. Make four hollows in mixture
and break eggs in. Cover and
leave to cook slowly for a further
3–5 minutes or until eggs are set.

===== COOK'S TIP =====

Whole eggs decorate the top of this
supper dish so try and use a
flameproof dish. The supper can
then go from cooker to table
without disturbing or breaking the
eggs. If using a frying pan then
carry pan to table using a heatproof
mat covered by a tea towel.

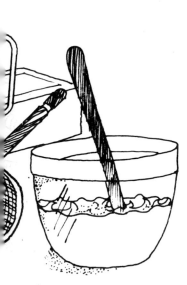

*Versatile savoury Bacon and beef △
roll is a meat loaf that can be
served hot or cold.*

*For a colourful way of serving ▷
bacon and eggs, try Farmhouse
supper dish.*

QUICHE LORRAINE

Serves 6

shortcrust pastry made with
   225g (8oz) flour (see Basic
   recipes, page 7)
5 medium eggs
175g (6oz) cheese, grated
salt and pepper
40g (1½oz) butter, melted
600ml (1 pint) creamy milk
1 small onion, finely chopped
   and lightly fried
100g (4oz) streaky bacon,
   chopped
sprig of parsley

1. Preheat oven to moderately
hot, 200°C (400°F) or gas 6.
2. Line a 30-cm (12-inch) flan tin
with pastry and prick the base.
3. Break the eggs into a bowl and
add the cheese, seasoning and
butter.
4. Whisk in the milk and add the
onion and the bacon.
5. Pour into the pastry case and
bake in centre of oven for
approximately 40 minutes or until
filling is puffy and golden brown.
6. Serve hot or cold garnished
with a sprig of parsley.

=== **COOK'S TIP** ===

If you use a pie plate rather than a
flan tin, it is important to get the
underneath pastry fully cooked in
the time the filling takes to set. Try
putting a baking tray into the oven
when starting to heat the oven. Put
the pie plate onto this hot tray and
continue cooking on it for the full
cooking time.
    You can vary the quiche by
adding asparagus tips or tuna fish
and shrimps.
    If you freeze the quiche, thaw
and heat it through before serving.

LITTLE CHICKEN PIES

Serves 6

3 chicken breasts
salt and pepper
50g (2oz) mushrooms, sliced
little flour to thicken
rough puff pastry made with
   175g (6oz) flour (see below)
1 small egg, beaten

1. Put the chicken in a pan; add
just enough water to cover, salt
and pepper and the mushrooms.
2. Bring to the boil then cover
pan and simmer for 1 hour, or
until chicken is tender; take meat
off bones.
3. Preheat oven to moderately hot,
200°C (400°F) or gas 6. Grease 6
patty tins.
4. Thicken the liquid from the
chicken with flour then mix
chicken pieces and mushrooms
back into it. Allow to cool.
5. Roll out pastry. Cut out 12
rounds. Use half to line tins.
Make leaves and stars from the
pastry trimmings.
6. Spoon the cooled chicken
mixture into the patty tins. Wet
edges of pastry; put on lids and seal.
7. Brush the tops with beaten egg
and make a small hole in the tops.
8. Brush pastry shapes with egg
and use to decorate the pies.
9. Bake, in the centre of the
preheated oven, for 25 minutes, or
until golden.

ROUGH PUFF PASTRY

Makes 175g (6oz) pastry

175g (6oz) plain flour
pinch of salt
110g (4oz) hard butter
¾ teaspoon lemon juice
cold water to mix

1. Sift flour and salt into a bowl.
2. Cut butter into small pieces,
about the size of a hazelnut.
3. Put butter in the mixing bowl.
Toss lightly with a spatula or
palette knife until butter is mixed
in and coated with flour.
4. Add the lemon juice and just
enough cold water to mix to a
light, fairly soft dough.
5. Roll out dough carefully into
an oblong.
6. Measure the oblong. Fold the
bottom third up over centre third
and fold top third down over
centre fold to make three layers.
7. Seal the edges with a rolling
pin. (It should not be necessary to
chill dough between rollings.)
8. Repeat the rolling and folding
process three times (giving the
dough a quarter turn before each
rolling and folding).
9. Wrap dough in foil and chill
for 1 hour before using.

△ *Quiche Lorraine is a classic
savoury flan. Serve with salad or
grilled tomatoes.*

◁ *Little chicken pies are excellent to
serve at a picnic or send in a
packed lunch as they transport
well.*

BACON AND EGG PLATE PIE

Serves 5

shortcrust pastry made with
 225g (8oz) flour (see Basic
 recipes, page 7)
5 lean back bacon rashers
4 medium eggs
salt and pepper
milk to glaze

1. Preheat oven to moderately hot, 200°C (400°F) or gas 6.
2. Roll out the pastry and use half of it to line a 18cm (7 inch) pie plate.
3. Take rind off bacon and chop the rashers.
4. Put chopped bacon in pastry-lined plate.
5. Break the eggs over the bacon so they are separate.
6. Season with salt and pepper, not too much.
7. Use rest of pastry to make a lid for the pie. Put in place.
8. Seal pastry edges and decorate with a knife, then press between thumb and forefinger to make flutes.
9. Use any trimmings to make leaves or any other decorative shapes for top of pie.
10. Brush the top with milk and make a small hole in the top of the pie.
11. Bake, in the centre of the preheated oven, for 20 minutes then reduce oven heat to moderate 180°C (350°F) or gas 4 for another 15 minutes or until brown.

CURRIED EGGS

Serves 4

4 hard-boiled eggs, shelled
4 tablespoons single cream
salt and pepper
2 level teaspoons curry paste
1 level dessertspoon chutney
 juice
shake of cayenne pepper
40g (1½oz) butter
2 small onions, chopped
1 garlic clove
1 level tablespoon curry
 powder
25g (1oz) flour
400ml (¾ pint) water
juice of ½ lemon
15g (½oz) sugar

1. Cut tops off eggs and scoop the yolks into a bowl.
2. Blend with cream, seasoning, 1 teaspoon curry paste, the chutney juice and cayenne pepper.
3. Fill mixture back into egg whites, replace tops and keep eggs warm.
4. Melt butter in a pan and add onions.
5. Crush and add garlic. Cook gently until tender and light golden, but not browned.
6. Mix in remaining curry paste and the curry powder and cook for a few more minutes.
7. Mix in flour and stir over heat until well blended.
8. Add water and season. Simmer for 20 minutes.
9. Blend in lemon juice and sugar.
10. Allow to heat through, then pour over eggs.
11. Serve on a bed of well-seasoned, boiled rice and garnish with chopped red and green peppers.

===== COOK'S TIP =====

These curried eggs are filled but eggs can be curried whole. Curries are better if left for up to 24 hours so that the flavours in the sauce mingle. Make the sauce in the morning and leave the eggs steeping in it. Reheat gently for supper while cooking the rice.

Filling Bacon and egg plate pie is △ a good and economical way to 'stretch' bacon and eggs.

Unlike meat and poultry curries, ▷ Curried eggs takes a very short time to prepare and cook.

KIDNEY TOASTS

Serves 4

500g (1lb) sheep's kidneys
salt and pepper
150ml (¼ pint) single cream
50g (2oz) flour
25g (1oz) lard
2 streaky bacon rashers,
    chopped
3 tomatoes, sliced
4 rounds of toast

1. Skin, core and slice the kidneys. Season well, dip them in cream and roll them in the flour.
2. Heat lard and fry the kidneys until until cooked through.
3. Add bacon in the last few moments.
4. Arrange tomato slices round the edge of a shallow serving dish.
5. Place toast in base of dish and pour kidney mixture over. Garnish with watercress and serve at once.

=== **COOK'S TIP** ===

You could use lambs' liver in this recipe and it would cook in the same time. Cut slices of liver into bite sized pieces before using as kidneys in the recipe.

HAM SUPPER

Serves 4

4 thick ham steaks or gammon
    rashers, about 2cm (¾ inch)
    thick
100g (4oz) demerara sugar
3 teaspoons dry mustard
300ml (½ pint) milk
cornflour

1. Preheat oven to moderately hot, 190°C (375°F) or gas 5.
2. Trim ham or gammon rashers and lay them in a casserole.
3. Sprinkle over 75g (3oz) sugar mixed with mustard.
4. Pour milk over and cover with a lid or piece of foil. Cook in centre of oven for 45 minutes.
5. Place ham or gammon on a shallow, ovenware dish.
6. Thicken sauce with cornflour and water paste.
7. Pour sauce over meat, sprinkle with remaining sugar and put under a hot grill.
8. Garnish with watercress and serve with a green salad.

=== **COOK'S TIP** ===

If you like fruit with ham, try pineapple, peaches, apricots or plums. The tartness of the fruit will contrast well with the crunchy sweet coating on the ham. Drain juice from the canned fruit and put in the dish with the ham for the final grilling. For an alternative fruit flavour, serve cranberry sauce separately.

△ *Well seasoned kidneys, dipped in cream, make Kidney toasts a quick but inventive supper dish when served with bacon and tomato on toast.*

◁ *Ham supper, served with a crisp green salad, takes about 1 hour to prepare and cook.*

Savouries and snacks

It's always snack time in a household, particularly with growing
children who like to have a snack when they come home from school.
Here are some quick, light and nourishing ideas. Also included are
savouries to serve as quick bites, appetizers or as cocktail or buffet food.
Cocktail savouries must be small, attractive and manageable to eat.

NORDIC DIP

Serves 4

100g (4oz) cream cheese
½ teaspoon paprika pepper
½ stick celery, chopped
50g (2oz) prawns, chopped
few drops Worcestershire
  sauce
salt and pepper
whole prawns to garnish
parsley

1. Mix the cream cheese with
paprika pepper, chopped celery
and chopped prawns. Add
Worcestershire sauce and
seasoning to taste.
2. Pile into a bowl and garnish
with whole prawns and parsley.
Sprinkle with paprika pepper and
serve with snack crackers or
potato crisps.

=== **COOK'S TIP** ===

To mix well, the cream cheese
should be at room temperature. Up
to 2 tablespoons single cream or top
of the milk added to the cream
cheese will soften the dip and make
it go a little further. Paprika
pepper is added for decoration and
is not hot. Cayenne pepper is red,
too, but is very hot and rarely used
for garnishing.

HOT SAUSAGES AND CHEESE DIP

Serves 4–6

500g (1lb) pork sausages
300ml (½ pint) thick white sauce
  (see Basic recipes, page 6)
225g (8oz) Cheddar cheese,
  grated
1 teaspoon made mustard
salt and pepper
150ml (¼ pint) single cream
4 tablespoons white wine
  (optional)

1. Twist each sausage into three
pieces. Grill until golden and keep
hot.
2. Warm the white sauce and stir
in the cheese and mustard.
3. Season well and add cream and
wine, if used.
4. Spike the sausages on cocktail
sticks and serve by dipping them
into the sauce.

=== **COOK'S TIP** ===

The white sauce must be thick.
Take care to measure all liquids
accurately, otherwise you will
have a sloppy dip that will drop
everywhere. Dry cider could
replace white wine.

△ *Creamy Nordic dip combines
cream cheese and prawns to make
an interesting starter or party dish.*

◁ *Serve celery and carrot sticks or
chunks of cucumber with super Hot
sausages and cheese dip.*

SAVOURY PORCUPINE

Serves 10

225g (8oz) chipolata sausages
50g (2oz) clear honey
few drops Worcestershire
  sauce
little dry mustard
50g (2oz) Cheddar cheese
75g (3oz) green grapes
1 can (187g or 7½oz) button
  mushrooms in brine
1 small can pineapple chunks
1 small firm cabbage

1. Prepare all the food before putting together the porcupine.
2. Keeping the sausages still in a string, twist each into two.
3. Heat the honey, Worcestershire sauce and mustard in a pan and, when it has melted, add the string of sausages.
4. Cook them gently, turning occasionally, for 20–30 minutes, until they are golden brown, cooked and glazed.
5. Drain on a wire tray.
6. Cut the cheese into 1cm (½ inch) cubes and wash the grapes.
7. Drain the mushrooms.
8. Cut the pineapple into smaller pieces if too large.
9. Remove any discoloured leaves from the cabbage and cut the base so the cabbage stands firm.
10. Arrange 16 cocktail sticks evenly around the cabbage, separate the sausages and spear one on to each stick.
11. Fill up the space between the sausages with cocktail sticks speared with a selection of the other ingredients – cheese and a grape, pineapple and mushroom.

=== COOK'S TIP ===

The porcupine body must be firm and sit well on the plate since it is party fare and guests will probably hold a glass in one hand and pull the savouries out with the other hand. A swede also works well but do not expect to use either vegetable again.

SEA SAVOURIES

Makes about 15

1 packet (75g or 3oz) cream
  cheese
1 can (225g or 8oz) pilchards in
  tomato sauce
pepper
small savoury biscuits
pickled cocktail onions or
  stuffed olives

1. Beat the cream cheese to a soft consistency.
2. Add the pilchards in tomato sauce and, using a fork, beat the mixture to a soft and pliable consistency. Season with pepper.
3. Place the filling in a large piping bag and pipe stars on to savoury biscuits.
4. Garnish with onions or slices of stuffed olive.

=== COOK'S TIP ===

Pilchards are a tasty fish and good in this savoury. After opening the can, pour contents onto a plate and, taking two forks, open up the body of the fish. Remove the backbone before beating the fish to a pulp.

Place delightful Savoury △ porcupine in the centre of a party spread.

An alternative filling for Sea ▷ savouries would be sardines in tomato sauce.

SAVOURY CHEESE BUNS

Makes 6

50g (2oz) Cheddar cheese, finely grated
choux pastry made with 65g (2½ oz) flour (see Basic recipes, page 7)
100g (4oz) cream cheese

1. Preheat oven to moderately hot, 200°C (400°F) or gas 6.
2. Beat 50g (2oz) of cheese into the choux pastry.
3. Spoon the mixture, in six large heaps, on a greased baking sheet.
4. Bake, in the centre of the preheated oven, for 15 minutes then reduce heat to moderate, 180°C (350°F) or gas 4 and bake for a further 35 minutes, or until dry.
5. Remove from the oven, split buns and remove any soft bits from inside.
6. Cool and fill with cream cheese.

CHEESE AIGRETTES

Makes 20

50g (2oz) Cheddar cheese, finely grated
choux pastry made with 65g (2½ oz) flour (see Basic recipes, page 7)
fat or oil for deep frying
coarsely grated cheese to garnish

1. Beat the cheese into the choux pastry.
2. Deep fry pastry in large spoonfuls in hot fat or oil, for 2–3 minutes until puffed up.
3. Drain well on absorbent kitchen paper.
4. Serve piled up and garnished with coarsely grated cheese.

═══ COOK'S TIP ═══

To cook cheese aigrettes successfully, it is important to test the heat of the fat with 1 teaspoon of the mixture before putting more into the pan. When cooked, the pastry ball will rise to the surface and needs to be turned for 1 minute. Remove all deep fried food when a light golden colour as appearance darkens slightly after cooking.

△ *Mouthwatering Savoury cheese buns filled with cream cheese make tempting buffet party fare.*

◁ *A delicious party snack, deep fried Cheese aigrettes should be served as soon as possible.*

CHEESE SAUSAGE ROLLS

Makes 8

cheese pastry made with 225g
(8oz) flour (see Basic recipes,
page 7)
8 slices processed cheese
8 frankfurter sausages
1 egg, beaten

1. Preheat oven to moderately
hot, 200°C (400°F) or gas 6.
2. Roll out the pastry and cut into
eight squares, slightly shorter
than the sausages.
3. Wrap a slice of cheese around
each sausage.
4. Wrap these in the pastry. Seal
edges with a little egg.
5. Brush each roll with egg.
6. Put on a baking sheet.
7. Bake, in centre of preheated
oven, for 20 minutes.

VOL-AU-VENTS

Makes 24

You will require 24 vol-au-vent
cases – they can be bought from
your baker ready made or frozen,
but uncooked, or you can make
them yourself. Make the fillings
early, put vol-au-vent cases on a
baking tray and fill at the last
minute. To serve hot, heat them
through in a moderate oven,
170°C (325°F) or gas 3, for about
15 minutes.

For the cases:
puff pastry made with 450g
(1lb) flour (see Basic recipes,
page 7)
little beaten egg to glaze

1. Preheat oven to hot, 230°C
(450°F) or gas 8.
2. Divide the pastry in two and
roll out each piece into a
rectangle 23 by 33cm (9 by 13
inches).
3. Using a 5cm (2 inch) fluted
cutter cut out 24 circles from each
piece.
4. Press a 2.5cm (1 inch) cutter
lightly into the centre of 24 of
them, but leave the centre in
position.

5. Brush the tops of the uncut
circles with a little water, lift a
marked pastry piece on top and
press the two circles together.
6. Put the cases on to baking
sheets and leave in a cool place
for 30 minutes.
7. Brush the tops with egg glaze
then bake near the top of the oven
for 8–10 minutes, until golden
brown and cooked. Cool on a wire
tray and remove the tiny centres.
8. Replace the centres after the
cases have been filled.

The fillings
Fillings for 24 cases. Each recipe
could be halved if two different
fillings are required.

HAM FILLING

225g (8oz) cooked ham shoulder
1 level dessertspoon piccalilli
600ml (1 pint) white sauce (see
Basic recipes, page 6)

1. Chop the ham finely and cut up
any large pieces in the piccalilli.
2. Stir these ingredients into the
sauce and check for seasoning.
3. Divide the filling between the
cases using a teaspoon.

HADDOCK AND TOMATO FILLING

350g (12oz) smoked haddock
fillet
3 large tomatoes
600ml (1 pint) white sauce (see
Basic recipes, page 6)
pinch of mace
salt and pepper

1. Wipe the fish, place it in
enough cold water to cover the
fillets and, over a very low heat,
bring the water to the boil.
2. Simmer the fish for about 5
minutes, then remove it from the
pan and place it on a plate.
3. Remove any skin and bones
and flake the fish.
4. Plunge the tomatoes into
boiling water for 20 seconds, then
transfer them to cold water and
peel off the skins.
5. Chop the tomatoes roughly and
mix them into the sauce with the
fish and the mace.
6. Check the filling for seasoning,
then divide it between the cases,
using a teaspoon for filling each
case.

*Savoury Cheese sausage rolls are △
made using rich cheese pastry;
ideal to serve at teenage parties.*

*Melt-in-the-mouth vol-au-vents are ▷
an ever popular savoury to serve at
all kinds of parties.*

STUFFED BACON ROLLS

Serves 4

8 back bacon rashers
2 onions
225g (8oz) mushrooms
50g (2oz) dripping
75g (3oz) breadcrumbs
2 teaspoons chopped parsley
salt and pepper
1 egg, beaten

1. Cut the rind off the bacon.
2. Skin the onions, chop with the mushrooms and fry gently in dripping.
3. Mix in the breadcrumbs and parsley.
4. Season well and bind with egg.
5. Spoon a little stuffing on to each rasher, roll up and secure with small skewers.
6. Grill on both sides until heated through and cooked.
7. Serve with potato crisps.

COOK'S TIP

You can make bacon more supple for stuffing or wrapping. First, have the bacon at room temperature for an hour. Put a slice on a board and, holding it down with one hand, use a spreading knife in the other. Press down and out as if spreading the bacon and the slice will grow and soften.

For another bacon-wrapped cocktail savoury, try using maraschino cherries. Drain a 225g (8oz) bottle of maraschino cherries. Cook 12–15 rashers of streaky bacon, derinded, until the fat is transparent and then cut each rasher into 2–3 pieces. Roll each piece of bacon round a cherry and arrange on skewers or spear with wooden cocktail sticks. Grill until crisp and golden on all sides. Remove from skewers, serve on cocktail sticks.

DEVILS ON HORSEBACK

Makes 15

1 can (425g or 15½oz) prunes
little sweet chutney
350g (12oz) streaky bacon rashers
watercress to garnish

1. Preheat oven to hot, 220°C (425°F) or gas 7.
2. Drain the prunes and carefully remove the stones.
3. Place a little chutney in the cavity left by the stone.
4. Cut the rind from the bacon and, with the back of a knife, stretch it to about double its original length.
5. Cut the bacon in half and wrap a piece around each prune.
6. Put the rolls into an ovenproof dish and cook in the centre of the oven for about 10 minutes, until the bacon is crisp.
7. Arrange in a dish and serve garnished with watercress. Have a small glass of cocktail sticks at hand to make eating them easier.

COOK'S TIP

When the stones are removed from the prunes, place a lightly fried blanched almond in each cavity. Devils on horseback may be served on 5cm (2 inch) rounds of fried bread.

△ *Interesting to serve Stuffed bacon rolls are filled with a tasty onion, mushroom and breadcrumb mixture.*

◁ *A classic, hot cocktail savoury, Devils on horseback combine the flavours of bacon and tender prunes.*

QUICK PIZZAS

Makes 12

6 baps or round soft rolls
175g (6oz) Cheddar cheese
150ml (¼ pint) tomato ketchup
150ml (¼ pint) water
1 level tablespoon made
    English mustard
salt and pepper
½ can anchovy fillets
1 small can prunes
parsley

1. Preheat the grill.
2. Cut each bap in half.
3. Coarsely grate the cheese into a bowl.
4. Stir in the tomato ketchup, water, mustard and seasoning.
5. Divide this mixture between the baps.
6. Smooth it almost to the sides it will spread during cooking.
7. Cut the anchovy fillets in half lengthways and the prunes into pieces, removing the stones.
8. Criss-cross the top of each pizza with the anchovies and garnish with pieces of prune.
9. Place under the grill until golden brown and bubbling.
10. Garnish with parsley sprigs and serve hot.

===== COOK'S TIP =====

As anchovies are canned in oil, they should be drained before use. They are also very salty so little extra salt is needed. To use up the remainder of the can, mash the fish with 15g (½oz) butter and spread on slices of hot toast for a snack.

SMORREBROD OR DANISH OPEN SANDWICHES

A national habit delightful for lunch or casual supper. The custom is said to have originated from the days when the poor served food on bread rather than plates. Various ingredients can be used, according to what is available, and the number of servings is also flexible.

BACON AND PÂTÉ

For each person allow:

20g (¾oz) pâté
1 slice wholemeal or rye bread,
    buttered
2 rolls grilled streaky bacon
3 or 4 button mushrooms,
    canned or fresh (if fresh,
    sauté in butter)
watercress

1. Spread the pâté on the bread.
2. Garnish with rolls of grilled bacon, button mushrooms and watercress.

CUCUMBER AND GHERKIN

For each person allow:

20g (¾oz) pâté
1 slice wholemeal or rye bread,
    buttered
1 sweet sour pickled gherkin,
    sliced into 4
4 cucumber, slices
1 radish, sliced
6 black olives, stoned

1. Spread the pâté on the bread.
2. Garnish with slices of gherkin, cucumber, radish and black olives.

Other interesting combinations are:
    A slice of ham and asparagus tips in mayonnaise.
    Sardines on cream cheese with green olives.
    Cream or cottage cheese on a slice of ham topped with orange slices.

Soft roll halves provide the bases of △ these colourful Quick pizzas; popular with everyone.

Attractive to look at and varied to ▷ eat, Smorrebrod are a classic Danish snack to serve any time.

SURPRISE SAVOURY LOAF

Serves 8

1 small French loaf
75g (3oz) butter
1 tablespoon salad cream
4 hard-boiled eggs
3 tomatoes
few lettuce leaves
salt and pepper

1. Split the loaf in half lengthways and remove enough of the bread from both pieces to hold the eggs and tomatoes.
2. Beat the butter and salad cream together and spread it over the inside of both pieces.
3. Shell and slice the eggs. Plunge the tomatoes into boiling water for 20 seconds, then transfer to cold water and peel off the skins; cut in slices.
4. Arrange the lettuce leaves in the bottom half of the loaf, place the egg and tomato slices down the centre and sprinkle with salt and pepper.
5. Replace the top of the loaf.
6. To serve, cut the loaf into thick slices.

===== COOK'S TIP =====

Many combinations of meat and salad can be used to fill a French loaf, but since it is bulky to eat do not use very soft fillings that will ooze out of the side. Ideas are:

Slices of cold roast pork with a little apple sauce, English mustard or chutney.

Slices of cold chicken and mayonnaise with a large pinch of curry powder.

Cream cheese liberally coated with salty chopped peanuts.

Always scoop out the centre of the loaf, spread with butter and top with lettuce before putting in the filling.

CRISPY STUFFED ROLLS

Serves 2

4 crisp dinner rolls
25g (1oz) butter
1 small onion
50g (2oz) mushrooms
3 tomatoes
3 eggs
salt and pepper

1. Preheat oven to moderate, 180°C (350°F) or gas 4.
2. Cut a round from top of each roll with a small plain pastry cutter or knife. Hollow out to leave a shell.
3. Melt butter, grate onion, chop mushrooms and peel and chop tomatoes.
4. Add vegetables to butter and fry gently for 5–10 minutes or until soft.
5. Beat eggs with seasoning, pour into pan and stir with a wooden spoon over a low heat until mixture thickens.
6. Pile filling into bread shells and replace rounds of bread to form lids.
7. Put on a baking sheet and cook in centre of oven for about 15 minutes, until rolls are crisp and filling heated through.

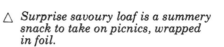

△ *Surprise savoury loaf is a summery snack to take on picnics, wrapped in foil.*

◁ *Filled with egg, tomato and mushrooms, Crispy stuffed rolls make a hot, satisfying snack lunch.*

CHEESY-BAKED POTATOES

Serves 6

3 medium potatoes
salt and pepper
25g (1oz) margarine
50g (2oz) mushrooms
50g (2oz) Cheddar cheese

1. Preheat oven to moderate, 180°C (350°F) or gas 4.
2. Scrub the potatoes, prick them all over with a fork and rub a little salt into the skins.
3. Place on a shelf of the oven and cook for 1½–2 hours, or until they are soft.
4. Melt half the margarine in a small pan, add the trimmed and sliced mushrooms and fry until tender.
5. When the potatoes are cooked, remove them from the oven and cut each one in half.
6. Using a spoon, scoop out the potato into a bowl and mix in the rest of the margarine with plenty of salt and pepper.
7. Put the potato skins on to a baking sheet and divide the cooked mushrooms between them, reserving a few to garnish.
8. Spoon the potato mixture on top, spreading out where necessary, then top with a little grated cheese and the reserved mushroom slices.
9. Reheat the potatoes required in a hot oven, 220°C (425°F) or gas 7, for about 15 minutes or until the cheese on top melts and is golden brown and crispy.

DUCHESSE EGG NESTS

Serves 4

500g (1lb) potatoes, cooked and mashed
25g (1oz) plain flour
3 eggs, beaten
salt and pepper
2 tablespoons milk
20g (¾oz) butter
25g (1oz) cheese, grated

1. Preheat oven to moderate, 180°C (350°F) or gas 4.
2. Shape the potato into four flat cakes and flour each lightly. Set them in a greased baking tin.
3. Hollow out the centres with a spoon.
4. Brush with a little beaten egg.
5. Bake for 15 minutes in centre of oven until golden and set.
6. Season the rest of the eggs, then add the milk.
7. Melt the butter in a saucepan and add the rest of the eggs.
8. Cook slowly, stirring, until set.
9. Pile into the potato nests.
10. Sprinkle with cheese and serve at once.

===== COOK'S TIP =====

Mashed potato in this recipe means only the potato without the milk or butter usually added when serving as a vegetable. The nests will then hold their shape. Put the nests in the tin before hollowing out the centre as they are likely to break up if moved.

Alternative fillings: any cooked leftover meat diced and put into a thick white sauce (see Basic recipes, page 6). Allow 175g (6oz) meat to 150ml (¼ pint) of the sauce and 2 tablespoons single cream or top of the milk.

Cheesy-baked potatoes combine the △
cooked potato with tangy cheese
and sautéed mushrooms.

For a more substantial snack, serve ▷
Duchesse egg nests with grilled
bacon or sausages.

CHEESE SQUARES

Serves 4

**approximately 1 litre (2 pints)
   milk
225g (8oz) semolina
100g (4oz) cheese, grated
75g (3oz) butter
2 egg yolks
salt and pepper
4 tomatoes
sprigs of watercress**

1. Preheat oven to moderately
hot, 200°C (400°F) or gas 6.
2. Bring milk to boil and sprinkle
in the semolina.
3. Stir over a gentle heat for 10
minutes until thickened.
4. Remove from heat and stir in
75g (3oz) grated cheese.
5. Add 15g (½oz) butter and egg
yolks. Season well.
6. Spread out on a plate and leave
to get cold. Cut into 2.5cm (1 inch)
squares.
7. Fill a pie dish with the squares
and tomato slices and top with
rest of cheese.
8. Bake in centre of oven dotted
with remaining butter for 15
minutes.
9. Garnish with watercress and
serve at once.

===== COOK'S TIP =====

Another name for this dish is
gnocchi. It comes from Rome and is
really an Italian version of
dumplings. To make it more
authentic, use Parmesan cheese for
the topping and serve with cooked
spinach. It can also be served as a
side dish in place of potatoes, rice
or noodles.

CHICKEN TURNOVERS

Makes 6

**flaky pastry made with 275g
   (10oz) flour (see Basic
   recipes, page 7)
3 large chicken pieces, cooked
15g (½oz) butter
15g (½oz) flour
150ml (¼ pint) milk
50g (2oz) cooked ham, minced
salt and pepper
1 egg, beaten**

1. Preheat oven to moderately
hot, 200°C (400°F) or gas 6.
2. Roll out the pastry to a large
square and cut into six equal-sized
squares.
3. Cut all the chicken meat off
and bones – it should be in fairly
small pieces.
4. Melt the butter in a small pan;
stir in the flour and cook gently,
stirring, for 2 minutes.
5. Whisk in the milk and bring to
the boil, stirring, until thickened.
6. Cook gently for 2 minutes then
stir in chicken and ham.
7. Season the mixture with salt
and pepper. Allow to cool.
8. Put some of the mixture in the
centre of each pastry square.
9. Brush pastry edges with egg
and fold over to make a triangle.
10. Brush triangles with egg.
11. Put the pastry on a baking
sheet.
12. Bake, in centre of preheated
oven, for 20–25 minutes, or until
golden.
13. These are good served hot or
cold.

△ *Cheese squares are made from a
cheese and semolina mixture. It is
cut in squares and baked until
crisp.*

◁ *Chicken turnovers are made with
light and delicate flaky pastry.*

Puddings and desserts

There are hot and cold puddings and desserts for all the seasons of the year. During the winter, puddings can afford to be more substantial and filling, while in summer light fruit desserts are best. Frozen or canned fruits play a large part in all these recipes.

BUTTERED FRUITS

Serves 8

**1 can (500g or 1lb) pineapple
    chunks
1 can (850g or 1lb 14oz) peach
    halves
1 can (500g or 1lb) apricot
    halves
50g (2oz) butter
175g (6oz) soft brown sugar
1 level teaspoon mixed spice
juice of half an orange
6 glacé cherries, halved**

1. Preheat oven to moderate,
180°C (350°F) or gas 4.
2. Drain fruits well. (The syrup
can be used to make a jelly.)
3. Arrange the fruits in a
casserole.
4. Melt butter in a pan and add
sugar, spice and orange juice. Mix
well together.
5. Sprinkle mixture over top of
fruit.
6. Cook below centre of oven for
45 minutes-1 hour, or until fruit is
heated through.
7. Decorate the top with glacé
cherries and serve hot with cream
or ice cream.

APRICOT SWEET

Serves 4

**500g (1lb) dried apricots
50g (2oz) caster sugar
suet crust pastry made with
    150g (5oz) flour (see Basic
    recipes, page 7)**

1. Put the apricots in a bowl,
cover with cold water and leave to
soak overnight.
2. Next day, put the fruit and
liquid in a pan.
3. Add sugar to pan and simmer
apricots gently for 30 minutes, or
until tender.
4. Liquidize or sieve fruit to make
a purée.
5. Form the pastry into fairly
large balls.
6. Drop these into a pan of gently
boiling water.
7. Put a lid on the pan and cook
dumplings for 15 minutes, or until
swollen and cooked.
8. Reheat apricot purée.
9. Put the hot purée in a dish;
top with dumplings and serve.

=== **COOK'S TIP** ===

These dumplings are made to serve
as a sweet and any purée of fruit
would do in place of apricots. A
suggested alternative is a purée of
rhubarb. To purée, cook fruit with
as little water as necessary to
prevent burning. Add sugar to taste
and sieve or liquidize. Use as
apricots in this recipe.

△ *Quickly prepared Buttered fruits is
a hot and spicy dessert which adds
sparkle to canned fruit.*

◁ *Serve warming, winter Apricot
sweet-apricot purée with
dumplings – with whipped cream
and brown sugar.*

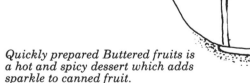

APRICOT CRUNCH

Serves 6

225g (8oz) dried apricots,
   washed well and soaked
   overnight
50g (2oz) sugar
15g (½oz) powdered gelatine
4 tablespoons water
1 small can evaporated milk,
   chilled
4 cartons (150ml or ¼ pint)
   natural yogurt
15g (½oz) butter
50g (2oz) demerara or raw sugar
50g (2oz) blanched almonds

1. Poach apricots with sugar for
20–25 minutes covered in water
used for soaking. Cover pan
during cooking
2. Drain, liquidize or sieve with 4
tablespoons cooking liquor.
3. Dissolve gelatine in 4
tablespoons water over a pan of
hot water.
4. Whisk chilled evaporated milk
till thick. Whisk in apricots and
gelatine. Stir in yogurt. Spoon
into dishes and chill till set.
5. Make topping by heating
butter and sugar gently in a pan
till sugar dissolves. Add chopped
almonds, mix well and leave to
cool. Crush and sprinkle on top.

===== COOK'S TIP =====

This dessert is very useful as dried
apricots can be bought all the year
round. Substitute a medium can of
apricots, drained if preferred. A
drop or two of pink food colouring
added at the last minute will ensure
a delicate pink that looks so
attractive under the crunchy
topping.

APRICOT FLAN

Serves 4–5

shortcrust pastry made with
   150g (5oz) flour (see Basic
   recipes, page 7)
300ml (½ pint) cold, thick,
   sweetened custard
rum to flavour
1 medium can apricot halves
150ml (¼ pint) double cream
   (optional)

1. Preheat oven to moderately
hot. 200°C (400°F) or gas 6.
2. Use the pastry to line a 18cm
(7 inch) flan tin and bake blind
(see page 7), in centre of
preheated oven for 20–25 minutes.
3. Leave pastry to cool.
4. Flavour the custard with the
rum.
5. Fill the flan with custard.
6. Drain juice off apricots (this is
not needed) and arrange the fruit,
rounded parts up, on top of the
custard.
7. If you are using cream, whip it
until it is thick and pipe it around
edge of flan or in between the
fruit.

===== COOK'S TIP =====

The drained juice can be used to
make a jelly. Measure juice and use
sufficient gelatine to set this
quantity according to instructions
on the packet. Add 2 or 3 drops of
orange food colouring before
allowing to set. Serve separately or
chop roughly with a knife and
spoon into gaps between apricots in
the flan.

*Mousse-like Apricot crunch is △
topped with a delicious mixture of
almonds and brown sugar.*

*Serve attractive Apricot flan as a ▷
dinner party dessert or at a
children's party.*

WEST COUNTRY PRUNES

Serves 4

225g (8oz) dried prunes
300ml (½ pint) sweet cider
4 tablespoons caster sugar
small strip of lemon rind
small piece of cinnamon stick

1. Soak prunes overnight in cider to cover.
2. Preheat oven to very moderate, 170°C (325°F) or gas 3.
3. Transfer prunes and cider to a small casserole and add sugar, lemon rind and cinnamon stick.
4. Cover closely with lid or foil and cook below centre of oven for about 40 minutes, or until prunes are tender.
5. Serve hot or cold with lightly whipped cream.

=== **COOK'S TIP** ===

Some prunes come in packets ready cooked, in which case soak in cider overnight adding lemon rind and cinnamon at this time. Serve cold after soaking overnight. To serve hot, bring to the boil and remove cinnamon stick.

STUFFED PEACHES

Serves 6

1 can (850g or 1lb 14oz) peach halves
2 tablespoons brandy
50g (2oz) ratafias, finely crushed, plus 4 whole ratafias for decoration
50g (2oz) ground almonds
1 level tablespoon caster sugar
150ml (¼ pint) double cream
strip of angelica

1. Preheat oven to moderately hot, 190°C (375°F) or gas 5.
2. Drain peaches, reserving the syrup, and arrange in a shallow, ovenproof dish.
3. Mix 150ml (¼ pint) reserved peach syrup with brandy and use a little of this to bind together the crushed ratafias and ground almonds.
4. Place a spoonful of the mixture in the hollow of each peach and sprinkle with a little sugar.
5. Pour remaining brandy syrup into the dish.
6. Cook, uncovered, above centre of oven for about 25 minutes.
7. Serve peaches hot with cream or chill and serve surrounded with piped whirls of whipped cream decorated with ratafias and chopped angelica.

=== **COOK'S TIP** ===

If ratafias are unobtainable, use one or two macaroons chopped with a cook's knife. Macaroons have a rice paper base and this can be left on during chopping. Decorate with whipped cream and angelica, omitting ratafias in this case.

△ *Rich tasting West Country prunes are cooked in a spicy cider in the oven.*

◁ *Hot stuffed peaches make an excellent entertaining dessert with a difference.*

ITALIAN STUFFED BAKED ORANGES

Serves 4

4 oranges
4–6 dates
few almonds or walnuts,
  chopped
3 tablespoons clear honey
2 tablespoons caster sugar
juice of 1 small lemon

1. Preheat oven to moderately hot, 190°C (375°F) or gas 5.
2. Peel oranges removing all pith. Place the oranges in a pan with some of the rind, cover with hot water and simmer for 30 minutes.
3. Remove from the water, save the liquid and cool. Core a deep hole in each orange.
4. Stone the dates.
5. Chop into small pieces and mix with almonds or walnuts, or a mixture of both.
6. Fill the orange holes with the date mixture and place in an ovenproof dish.
7. Boil 400ml (¾ pint) of the orange water, the honey and sugar together for 2–3 minutes.
8. Add lemon juice and pour over the oranges.
9. Bake for 1 hour, spooning over the syrup occasionally.
10. Cool and chill. Serve very cold. (This can be turned into a spectacular dessert by placing a sugar cube. which has been dipped in brandy, on each orange and igniting them at table.)

SHERRY-BAKED BANANAS

Serves 4

6 bananas, preferably soft
150ml (¼ pint) medium sherry
75g (3oz) demerara or raw
  sugar
20g (¾oz) butter
whipped cream and sponge
  fingers to serve

1. Preheat oven to moderately hot, 190°C (375°F) or gas 5.
2. Peel bananas, cut in a half down the centre and place in a shallow, ovenproof dish.
3. Pour sherry over, sprinkle with sugar and dot with butter.
4. Bake in centre of oven for 25 minutes.
5. Serve piping hot with whipped cream and sponge fingers.

A medieval dessert, Italian △ stuffed baked oranges were first served in Venice 400 years ago.

When you want to serve a hot ▷ pudding and there is little time, prepare tempting Sherry-baked bananas.

SPIKED APPLES

Serves 4

4 cooking apples, peeled, halved and cored
75g (3oz) demerara or raw sugar
50g (2oz) chopped candied peel
600ml (1 pint) cider or unsweetened apple juice
50g (2oz) almonds, blanched and cut into spikes

1. Preheat oven to moderate, 180°C (350°F) or gas 4.
2. Arrange apples in a shallow casserole. Sprinkle with sugar, scatter with peel and pour cider or apple juice over.
3. Cover with lid or foil and cook towards base of oven for about 1 hour, or until apples are tender but still retain their shape.
4. Transfer apples carefully to a serving dish and spike with almonds.
5. Pour liquid from the dish into a pan, boil until well reduced, then pour over the apples.
6. Serve hot or cold with cream or custard.

===== COOK'S TIP =====

An alternative fruit for this would be pears, especially the varieties available in the winter that are sometimes hard. Use 50g (2oz) candied or preserved ginger chopped instead of candied peel and proceed as the recipe.

APPLE DUMPLINGS

Makes 4

shortcrust pastry made with 450g (1lb) flour (see Basic recipes, page 7)
4 large cooking apples
50g (2oz) brown sugar
25g (1oz) butter
milk to glaze

1. Preheat oven to moderately hot, 200°C (400°F) or gas 6.
2. Roll out the pastry and cut into four large rounds. Make leaves from the trimmings.
3. Peel the apples and remove the cores.
4. Mix the sugar with the butter and use to fill centre of each apple.
5. Mould pastry round each apple so that it is enclosed.
6. Decorate each one with the pastry leaves and brush with milk.
7. Put apple dumplings on a baking sheet and bake, in centre of preheated oven, for 15 minutes.
8. Turn oven down to moderate, 180°C (350°F) or gas 4, and cook for another 50 minutes, covering pastry with foil if it becomes too brown.

△ *Apples baked in cider and decorated, hedgehog fashion, with almonds make Spiked apples a fun dessert.*

◁ *Satisfying baked Apple dumplings are whole sweetened apples wrapped in crisp and light shortcrust pastry.*

FLAN AUX POMMES

Serves 4–6

shortcrust pastry made with
  100g (4oz) flour (see Basic
  recipes, page 7)
500g (1lb) cooking apples
150ml (¼ pint) white wine
2 tablespoons water
50g (2oz) sugar
2 eating apples
juice of 1 lemon
1 glacé cherry

1. Preheat oven to moderately hot,
200°C (400°F) or gas 6.
2. Roll out and line a 19 cm (7½
inch) flan ring with pastry.
3. Prick pastry with a fork.
4. Bake blind (see page 7) in
centre of preheated oven for 15
minutes.
5. Peel and slice cooking apples
into a pan.
6. Add wine, water and sugar and
cook slowly until tender.
7. Drain and spoon into pastry
cases.
8. Core and slice eating apples
and dip in lemon juice.
9. Arrange over the top of the
flan.
10. Return to the oven for a
further 5 minutes.
11. Decorate with a glacé cherry
in the centre and serve hot or
cold.

SUMMER FLAN

Serves 4

shortcrust pastry made with
  150g (5oz) flour (see Basic
  recipes, page 7)
½ packet raspberry jelly
300ml (½ pint) double cream
1 small can raspberries,
  drained
little fresh or frozen fruit to
  decorate (optional)

1. Preheat oven to moderately
hot, 200°C (400°F) or gas 6.
2. Roll out pastry and use to line
an 18cm (7 inch) flan ring, or
sandwich tin with a loose base.
3. Prick pastry with a fork.
4. Bake blind (see page 7), in
centre of preheated oven, for
20–25 minutes, or until golden.
Leave to cool.
5. Make up jelly as directed on
the packet, but use half the
amount of water.
6. Leave jelly in cold place until
it is beginning to set round the
edges then pour into the pastry
flan. Smooth top and leave to set.
7. Whip the cream until thick but
not buttery.
8. Fold the drained canned fruit
into the cream.
9. Spoon this on top of jelly.
10. Decorate with fresh or frozen
fruit.

═══ COOK'S TIP ═══

This recipe uses canned raspberries
but any fruit could be substituted.
Fresh soft fruit such as
strawberries, blackcurrants,
loganberries and blackberries
would be particularly suitable, or a
mixture such as raspberry and
redcurrant. If using fresh fruit,
leave some aside for decoration and
cook remainder in enough water to
cover. Sweeten to taste. Drain off
liquid and use this to make the
jelly. Fold the cooked fruit into the
whipped cream and spoon on top of
jelly in pastry case. Decorate with
the reserved fresh fruit.

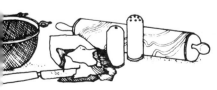

A classic French tart, Flan aux △
*pommes makes an impressive
dinner party dessert.*

Luscious Summer flan combines ▷
*the soft fruits of summer with fresh
cream in a pastry case.*

SPONGE FLAN

Serves 6

75g (3oz) self-raising flour
100g (4oz) margarine
75g (3oz) caster sugar
2 medium eggs
1 tablespoon warm water
1 can (500g or 1lb) red plums
arrowroot, to thicken
50g (2oz) icing sugar

1. Preheat oven to moderate, 180°C (350°F) or gas 4.
2. Grease and lightly flour a 20cm (8 inch) sponge flan tin.
3. Sift the flour into a bowl.
4. In another bowl, cream 75g (3oz) margarine with the caster sugar until light and fluffy.
5. Beat in one egg. Separate the other egg and beat yolk into mixture. (The egg white is not needed.)
6. Using a metal spoon, fold the flour and warm water into the mixture.
7. Spoon mixture into prepared tin; smooth the top.
8. Bake in centre of preheated oven for 25 minutes or until firm to the touch.
9. Leave the cake to cool in tin for 3 minutes then turn out to cool on a wire rack.
10. Drain the fruit and reserve the juice.
11. Arrange the fruit in the flan case.
12. Following the instructions on the packet, thicken the fruit juice with arrowroot. When mixture is nearly cold, spoon it on top of the fruit.
13. Beat the rest of the margarine with the icing sugar until light and fluffy.
14. Put this mixture in a piping bag fitted with a small star nozzle and pipe neat stars round top edge and base of flan.

PLUM PIE

Serves 4

shortcrust pastry made with 175g (6oz) flour (see Basic recipes, page 7)
1 large can red plums or 500g (1lb) stewed fresh fruit
arrowroot to thicken
25g (1oz) caster sugar

1. Preheat oven to moderately hot, 200°C (400°F) or gas 6.
2. Roll out the pastry to a large circle. Cut off a 2.5cm (1 inch) wide strip and put it all round the edge of a 1 litre (1½ pint) pie dish.
3. Drain the juice off the fruit and thicken it with the arrowroot, as instructed on the packet.
4. Stir the fruit back into the juice and add to pie dish.
5. Trim the pastry circle and use to cover pie, moistening pastry edge before putting lid on.
6. Make half circles and leaves from the trimmings and use to decorate the top.
7. Make a small hole in centre.
8. Bake, in centre of preheated oven, for 15 minutes.
9. Reduce heat to moderate, 180°C (350°F) or gas 4, and cook pie for a further 30 minutes or until golden brown.
10. Sprinkle caster sugar over the top and serve hot or cold.

COOK'S TIP

Try adding ½ teaspoon powdered cinnamon to the arrowroot when thickening the liquid from the fruit; the flavour goes well with plums. Always cool any filling thoroughly before covering with pastry or the steam rising from the warm filling will make the pastry soft. This applies to both sweet and savoury pies where the filling is cooked before being topped by pastry, such as steak and kidney pie.

△ *The sponge base of pretty Sponge flan can be made the day before and stored in an airtight tin.*

◁ *Homely Plum pie is a favourite pudding to serve in the cold, winter months.*

FRUIT RING

Serves 4–5

**puff pastry made with 225g
   (8oz) flour (see Basic recipes,
   page 7)**
100g (4oz) dates, chopped
50g (2oz) raisins
**50g (2oz) glacé cherries,
   chopped**
2 tablespoons clear honey
2 tablespoons lemon juice
caster sugar to sprinkle

1. Preheat oven to moderately
hot, 200°C (400°F) or gas 6.
2. Roll out the pastry into a long
wide strip.
3. Brush the edges of the pastry
with water.
4. Mix the fruit with the honey
and lemon juice.
5. Spoon this mixture on to the
pastry, leaving at least 2.5cm
(1 inch) clear all round the edge.
6. Roll up lengthwise, just like a
Swiss roll. Seal the edges.
7. Join the edges to make a ring.
8. Put on a baking sheet.
9. Working on the outside of the
ring, snip the pastry at 5cm (2
inch) intervals.
10. Bake, in centre of preheated
oven, for 25 minutes, or until
golden brown.
11. Sprinkle with sugar and serve
hot with cream.

=== **COOK'S TIP** ===

To measure honey or syrup more
accurately, use a heated spoon. It
must be a metal spoon and can be
heated in boiling water or directly
in a gas flame for a few seconds to
warm thoroughly. Dip into honey
or syrup and the warmth will cut
through the thick liquid, making it
easier to get a level measurement.

FRUITY CHEESE
CAKE

Serves 4–6

**shortcrust pastry made with
   100g (4oz) flour (see Basic
   recipes, page 7)**
**1 can (225g or 8oz) pineapple
   pieces**
50g (2oz) sultanas
50g (2oz) raisins
**grated rind and juice of
   1 lemon**
150ml (¼ pint) single cream
1 egg, lightly beaten
25g (1oz) butter
50g (2oz) caster sugar

1. Preheat oven to hot, 220°C
(425°F) or gas 7.
2. Roll out pastry and line an 18cm
(7 inch) flan ring. Prick base and
bake blind (see page 7) in centre
of oven for 10 minutes.
3. Lower oven setting to very
moderate, 170°C (325°F) or gas 3.
4. Drain pineapple. Coarsely chop
pieces and mix with sultanas,
raisins and lemon rind.
5. Spread mixture over base of
baked pastry case.
6. Mix lemon juice, cream and
egg together. Cream butter and
sugar till fluffy. Add to cream
mixture.
7. Blend well together, pour over
fruit and bake in centre of oven
for 30–40 minutes till set. Serve
hot or cold.

=== **COOK'S TIP** ===

This recipe does not contain cream
cheese or cottage cheese as the
name might suggest. However, it is
a very tasty recipe and well worth
trying. Fruit at the bottom of a
pastry case is covered and cooked
with a topping of cream, egg, lemon
juice, butter and sugar.

*Dates, raisins, glacé cherries and △
honey wrapped in puff pastry make
the mouthwatering Fruit ring.*

*Baked Fruity cheese cake combines ▷
pineapple and dried fruits with a
creamy topping.*

CRUNCHY LEMON PIE

Serves 4–6

100g (4oz) butter
100g (4oz) sugar
175g (6oz) digestive biscuits, crushed with a rolling pin
1 level tablespoon gelatine
4 tablespoons water
150ml (¼ pint) lemon juice
4 eggs, separated
225g (8oz) caster sugar
salt
2 teaspoons cornflour
chopped nuts
green food colouring
150ml (¼ pint) double cream, whipped

1. Melt butter and sugar in a saucepan.
2. Stir in the biscuit crumbs.
3. Mix well together and press the mixture into a 20cm (8 inch) pie plate.
4. Chill until firm.
5. Dissolve gelatine in water over a low heat.
6. Blend with lemon juice, egg yolks, half the sugar, the salt and cornflour.
7. Cook gently over a pan of hot water until mixture thickens slightly.
8. Leave in a cool place until nearly set.
9. Whisk egg whites until stiff enough to stand in peaks.
10. Add remaining sugar and fold into the lemon mixture.
11. Spoon into the crumb case and chill.
12. Mix nuts with a few drops of green food colouring and sprinkle them over the pie.
13. Decorate with whipped cream and serve.

BLACKBERRY MERINGUE PIE

Serves 4–5

shortcrust pastry made with 150g (5oz) flour (see Basic recipes, page 7)
2 small cans blackberries or 500g (1lb) stewed and sweetened fresh fruit
arrowroot to thicken
1 large egg white
50g (2oz) caster sugar

1. Preheat oven to 200°C (400°F) or gas 6.
2. Use the pastry to line an 18cm (7 inch) flan case and bake blind (see page 7), for 15 minutes. Leave oven on.
3. Drain the juice off the fruit and thicken it with arrowroot, following instructions on the packet.
4. Mix the fruit back into the juice and spoon into the cooked pastry flan.
5. Whisk the egg white until very stiff.
6. Whisk in half the sugar then fold in the rest and spoon on top of the fruit.
7. Return to the centre of the preheated oven for 15–20 minutes, or until the meringue is a pale golden colour.
8. Serve at once.

═══ COOK'S TIP ═══

Meringue cooked on top of a pie like this is cooked fairly rapidly to give a crisp outside and a softer inside. Be sure to spread the meringue right over the fruit filling to join the pastry. Watch timing carefully as the meringue may brown in less than 20 minutes. The pie can be served cold but this meringue topping is best served the same day.

△ *Delightful Crunchy lemon pie has a biscuit crumb base. Other biscuits like gingernuts may be used.*

◁ *Spectacular Blackberry meringue pie provides the contrasting textures of pastry, fruit and meringue.*

COFFEE MERINGUE GATEAU

Serves 6

4 large egg whites
2 tablespoons coffee essence
225g (8oz) caster sugar
300ml (½ pint) double cream
150ml (¼ pint) single cream
3 bananas
juice of half a lemon
little extra icing sugar
few coffee sugar crystals

1. Preheat oven to cool, 150°C (300°F) or gas 2.
2. Put the egg whites, coffee essence and sugar into a bowl and place it over a pan of hot water.
3. Whisk for about 10 minutes, or until the mixture is stiff and shiny. (If you use an electric mixer there is no need to place the bowl over hot water.)
4. Remove from the heat and whisk for 2 more minutes.
5. Cover two baking sheets with bakewell paper.
6. Fill a piping bag with the mixture and pipe on to each tray a 20cm (8 inch) circle.
7. Sprinkle the rounds with caster sugar then bake them for 1½–2 hours, until completely dry. Cool on a wire tray.
8. Whip the creams together until they hold their shape.
9. Place one round of meringue on a serving dish and spread over most of the cream.
10. Peel and slice the bananas, toss in lemon juice and arrange on top of the cream.
11. Place the other round on top.
12. Put the rest of the cream into a piping bag.
13. Sprinkle the surface of the gâteau with icing sugar, then pipe swirls of cream around the edge.
14. Sprinkle coffee sugar crystals on each swirl.

=== **COOK'S TIP** ===

These meringues for the coffee gâteau are cooked much longer than for a meringue pie topping and need to be dried right through. If your oven cooks dishes quickly then turn down temperature to 140°C (275°F) or gas 1. Meringues will not store well unless thoroughly cooked.

Of course, meringues make melt-in-the-mouth cakes in their own right. Pipe 5cm (2 inch) swirls of meringue mixture onto paper-lined baking sheets and bake as recipe. Sandwich two swirls with whipped cream flavoured with crushed fruit, jam, liqueur or clear honey.

PEACH MERINGUE SURPRISE

Serves 5

3 large egg whites
175g (6oz) caster sugar
1 heaped teaspoon cornflour
1 teaspoon white vinegar
a little vanilla essence
1 can (425g or 15oz) peach halves
150ml (¼ pint) cold, thick custard

1. Preheat oven to cool, 150°C (300°F) or gas 2.
2. Grease a 30cm (12 inch) piece of foil. Put the foil on a baking sheet.
3. Whisk the egg whites until very stiff.
4. Very gradually whisk in the sugar.
5. Using a metal spoon, fold cornflour into whisked mixture with the vinegar and vanilla essence.
6. Put half of the meringue in a piping bag fitted with a large plain nozzle. Pipe a thick ring of meringue on the foil.
7. Spread half of the rest of the meringue in the centre of the circle, so you have made a basket shape. Use rest of meringue to pipe a 'wall' on basket, so making a fairly deep case.
8. Bake in the centre of the preheated oven for 45 minutes, or until firm. (The meringue should be like marshmallow under its firm top coating.)
9. Leave meringue to cool.
10. Drain the fruit. The juice will not be needed.
11. Chop or mince half the fruit and stir it into the custard.
12. Fill the cooled meringue with custard mixture, then top with the remaining pieces of fruit, rounded sides up.

=== **COOK'S TIP** ===

This cake should be assembled just before serving, but the meringue can be made the day before. If the filling is put in too early it will soften the meringue, thus making serving difficult.

Assemble fabulous Coffee △ meringue gâteau only 2 hours before it is to be eaten.

An attractive party dessert, make ▷ the meringue nest for Peach meringue surprise in advance.

SYLLABUB TREAT

Serves 4–5

**shortcrust pastry made with
150g (5oz) flour (see Basic
recipes, page 7)**
300ml (½ pint) double cream
little Madeira
4 tablespoons white wine
**grated rind and juice of half a
small lemon**
100g (4oz) green grapes
**fresh or crystallized lemon
slices to decorate**

1. Preheat oven to moderately
hot, 200°C (400°F) or gas 6.
2. Use pastry to line an 18cm (7
inch) flan ring or oval dish 20cm
(8 inches) long. Bake blind (see
page 7) in centre of preheated
oven for 20–25 minutes.
3. Leave pastry to cool.
4. Whip the cream.
5. Mix the Madeira, wine, lemon
juice and rind into the cream.
6. Put the grapes in the base of
the flan.
7. Pipe the cream in circles on top
of the grapes or spoon it on and
mark ridges with a fork.
8. Decorate with fresh or
crystallized lemon slices.

HAGUE'S BLUFF

Serves 4–6

12 tablespoons raspberry syrup
225g (8oz) sugar or to taste
4 egg whites

1. Put syrup, sugar and unbeaten
egg whites in a large bowl.
2. Whisk for 10 minutes or more
(if by hand) to increase the
amount.
3. Serve in individual dishes with
wafers or sponge finger biscuits.

═══ COOK'S TIP ═══

A very simple dessert which is light
to serve at a party when the
previous courses have been
heartier. Try bottled blackcurrant
juice in place of raspberry syrup; it
has a good strong flavour and
makes a pretty pink colour. If using
syrup from frozen fruit then use the
drained fruit under the Bluff in
individual serving dishes.
Loganberries or redcurrants would
also give a good flavour.

△ *Rich Syllabub treat blends the
flavours of Madeira, wine, cream
and grapes in a crisp pastry case.*

◁ *A Dutch dessert, Hague's bluff
makes a fluffy sweet out of few
ingredients.*

OLD DANISH RUM PUDDING

Serves 4

2 egg yolks
65g (2½oz) granulated sugar
25g (1oz) vanilla sugar
1 small glass rum
300ml (½ pint) milk
3 level teaspoons powdered gelatine dissolved in 1 tablespoon hot water
150ml (¼ pint) whipping cream
1 can (225g or 8oz) Morello cherries
4 tablespoons water
1 level tablespoon cornflour

1. Whisk the egg yolks, sugar, vanilla sugar and rum in a bowl until thick and frothy.
2. Meanwhile, heat the milk and when it boils, gradually pour it into the egg mixture.
3. Stir in the dissolved gelatine.
4. Leave in a cool place until the rum custard is cold.
5. Whip pre-chilled cream and fold into the rum custard. Pour into a rinsed mould and leave to set.
6. Empty contents of can of cherries into a pan; add half the water and bring to the boil.
7. Dissolve cornflour in remaining water and add to the cherries, stirring.
8. Boil for 2–3 minutes over gentle heat, then leave to cool slightly, and pour over the unmoulded pudding.

=== **COOK'S TIP** ===

Vanilla sugar can be bought in small packets but you can make you own in two ways. The first is quick: add ½ teaspoon vanilla essence to 25g (1oz) sugar. The second method requires a vanilla pod, which is long and black, rather like a bean pod and available in specialist grocery shops. Fill a jar a little taller than the length of the pod with caster sugar. Put the pod in middle and put on lid tightly. Leave for 1 week to infuse, then use sugar as required. Replace sugar used in jar. The pod will gradually lose its strength and must be replaced.

CHOCOLATE MOUSSE

Serves 4

100g (4oz) milk or plain chocolate
4 eggs, separated
double cream and grated chocolate to decorate

1. Melt chocolate with 4 teaspoons water in a thick saucepan, over a very low heat.
2. Remove from heat and beat in egg yolks.
3. Let mixture cool slightly.
4. Whisk egg whites until soft peaks form. Fold into the chocolate.
5. Pour into individual dishes and leave to set. Decorate with whipped cream and grated chocolate.

A rich, creamy, cold sweet, Old Danish rum pudding is served with cherry sauce. △

Ever popular Chocolate mousse finishes a dinner party in the best way possible. ▷

BANANA CREAM SANDWICH

Serves 6

40g (1½oz) plain flour
pinch of salt
1 level teaspoon baking powder
225g (8oz) medium oatmeal
25g (1oz) caster sugar
50g (2oz) margarine
milk to mix
2 large ripe bananas
2 tablespoons double cream

1. Preheat oven to very moderate, 170°C (325°F) or gas 3.
2. Grease two baking sheets.
3. Sift the flour with the salt and baking powder in a bowl.
4. Mix in the oatmeal and sugar.
5. Cut the margarine into small pieces and rub into flour until mixture resembles fine breadcrumbs.
6. Add enough milk to mix to a stiff dough.
7. Sprinkle working surface with a little flour and oatmeal, mixed.
8. Roll out dough on working surface to about 5mm (¼ inch) thick.
9. Using a large saucer as a guide, cut out three rounds from the dough.
10. Put the rounds on baking sheets.
11. Bake in the centre of the preheated oven for 35 minutes, or until golden brown and crisp.
12. Put to cool on a wire rack.
13. Peel and mash the bananas and mix them with the cream.
14. Sandwich the rounds with the banana mixture and serve the same day.

SPANISH CHOCOLATE FRIED BREAD

Serves 4

stale bread slices, 1cm (½ inch) thick
1 egg yolk
300ml (½ pint) milk
1 tablespoon sherry
butter for frying
caster sugar
grated chocolate

1. Cut the bread into fingers about 2.5cm (1 inch) wide.
2. Beat the egg yolk and add the milk and sherry.
3. Dip the bread into this, drain and fry until golden in the butter.
4. Drain on absorbent paper, sprinkle with caster sugar and cover with grated chocolate, reserving some to decorate.
5. Pile on to a dish and sprinkle with chocolate
6. Serve very hot.

=== **COOK'S TIP** ===

This is an excellent way of using up stale bread and could be served at brunch or for breakfast as well as a sweet. Use the fried bread with warmed jam, maple syrup or warmed apple sauce in place of chocolate. A sprinkling of cinnamon and brown sugar also goes well.

△ *Tempting Banana cream sandwich is a cake-like dessert filled with mashed bananas and cream.*

◁ *Spanish chocolate fried bread are fingers of fried bread sprinkled with chocolate – a hit with children.*

Cakes
and baking

There is something satisfying about spending a morning or afternoon
baking and nothing nicer than coming into the house and smelling the
results. Baking two and freezing one can be the answer for busy people,
and there are plain and fancy cakes and biscuits for you here.

DRIPPING CAKE

Serves about 6

350g (12oz) self-raising flour
pinch of salt
110g (4oz) dripping
125g (4½oz) caster sugar, plus a
    little extra
175g (6oz) sultanas
1 large egg
5 tablespoons milk

1. Preheat oven to moderately
hot, 190°C (375°F) or gas 5.
2. Grease and line the base of an
18cm (7 inch) round, deep cake
tin.
3. Sift flour and salt into a bowl.
4. Cut the dripping up a little and
rub it into the flour until mixture
resembles fine breadcrumbs.
5. Stir in 110g (4oz) caster sugar
and the sultanas.
6. Beat the egg with the milk.
7. Stir enough egg and milk into
rubbed-in mixture to make a stiff
dough.
8. Put in prepared tin and press
down lightly.
9. Sprinkle rest of sugar over top
of cake.
10. Bake in centre of preheated
oven for 1 hour 10 minutes, then
test by inserting the warmed
blade of a knife into the cake. If
the cake is done the knife blade
will be clean when withdrawn. If
not, cook a little longer, then test
again in the same way.
11. Turn out to cool on a wire
rack. Sprinkle on extra sugar.
12. Store cake in an airtight tin.

═══ COOK'S TIP ═══

This an economical cake which
travels well for picnics or school
lunches. Use margarine in the
recipe in place of dripping, if
preferred, and any mixture of dried
fruit can replace the sultanas.
   To clarify dripping (separate it
from meat bits and juices) put it in
a dish, and pour boiling water on
top and leave it in the refrigerator
overnight. Next day, lift layer of
dripping off top. The sediment will
have sunk to base of dish.

FRUIT-TOPPED LOAF

Serves about 6

450g (1lb) plain flour
110g (4oz) margarine
20g (¾oz) fresh yeast
150ml (¼ pint) tepid milk
150ml (¼ pint) tepid water
1 medium egg, beaten
pinch of salt
110g (4oz) caster sugar
75g (3oz) currants
50g (2oz) glacé cherries
25g (1oz) angelica or green
    glacé cherries
2 teaspoons golden syrup or
    clear honey

1. Sift the flour into a mixing
bowl.
2. Rub the margarine into the
flour until mixture resembles fine
breadcrumbs.
3. Cream the yeast with a little of
the tepid milk. Stir in rest of milk,
tepid water and egg.
4. Add yeast liquid to flour.
4. Mix well then knead for at
least 5 minutes, or until the dough
is smooth and elastic and leaves
your fingers and the sides of the
bowl clean.
6. Lightly grease or oil the inside
of a large polythene bag.
7. Slip the bowl of dough into the
bag.
8. Leave the dough in a warm
place – not near direct heat or
boiler – for 1½ hours, or until
dough has doubled in size.
9. Remove from bag. Knead the
salt, sugar and currants into the
risen dough.
10. Put the dough in two greased
loaf tins each 15cm (6 inches) by
10cm (4 inches) by 7.5cm (3
inches).
11. Leave the dough in a warm
place to prove (rise again) for 15
minutes.
12. Preheat oven to hot, 220°C
(425°F) or gas 7.
13. Bake the loaves in the centre
of the preheated oven for 30
minutes or until well risen and
firm. When the bread is tapped on
the base it should sound hollow.
14. Leave to cool completely.
15. Chop up the cherries and
angelica fairly finely. Mix them
with the syrup. Spoon on top of
the loaves.

△ *A simple to make fruit cake, eat
homely Dripping cake within 3
days.*

◁ *Yeasty Fruit-topped loaf contains
currants and, when baked, a
mixture of glacé cherries, angelica
and golden syrup is spread on top.*

MARMALADE LOAF

Serves about 6

110g (4oz) margarine
450g (1lb) plain flour
20g ($\frac{3}{4}$oz) fresh yeast
150ml ($\frac{1}{4}$ pint) tepid milk
150ml ($\frac{1}{4}$ pint) tepid water
1 medium egg, beaten
pinch of salt
110g (4oz) caster sugar
75g (3oz) currants
150g (5oz) rough-cut
    marmalade

1. Sift the flour into a mixing bowl.
2. Rub the margarine into the flour.
3. Cream the yeast with a little of the tepid milk, then mix with rest of tepid liquids and the egg.
4. Make a well in the centre of the flour and add the yeast liquid.
5. Mix well then knead for at least 5 minutes until the dough is smooth and elastic and leaves your fingers and the sides of the bowl clean.
6. Lightly grease or oil the inside of a large polythene bag.
7. Slip the bowl of dough inside the polythene bag and leave for 1$\frac{1}{2}$ hours in a warm place – not near direct heat, or boiler – or until dough has risen to twice its size.
8. Remove from bag. Knead the salt, sugar and currants into the risen dough.
9. Separate about half the peel from the marmalade. Chop this and knead it into the dough.
10. Put the dough into two greased loaf tins, each 15cm (6 inches) by 10cm (4 inches) by 7.5cm (3 inches) and leave to prove (rise again) for 15 minutes, or until the dough has risen to the top of the tins.
11. Preheat oven to hot, 220°C (425°F) or gas 7.
12. Bake the loaves in the centre of the preheated oven for 30 minutes or until well risen; the loaves should sound hollow when tapped on the base.
13. Leave to cool completely.
14. Top loaves with rest of marmalade and serve sliced and buttered, with more marmalade.

=== **COOK'S TIP** ===

Yeast mixtures freeze well, so this would be a good recipe to make and freeze one loaf, or double the quantity and freeze three loaves. Remember to put date and contents clearly on the outside of freezer packages.

CHERRY PLAIT

Serves 4–5

25g (1oz) margarine
225g (8oz) plain flour
15g ($\frac{1}{2}$oz) fresh yeast
4 tablespoons tepid milk
4 tablespoons tepid water
1 small egg, beaten
40g (1$\frac{1}{2}$oz) caster sugar
pinch of salt
50g (2oz) icing sugar, sifted
3 glacé cherries

1. Sift the flour into a bowl.
2. Rub in the margarine.
3. Cream the yeast with a little of the tepid milk then mix with the rest of the milk and water.
4. Make a well in the centre of the flour and add the yeast liquid and the egg. Mix well.
5. Knead for 5 minutes, or until the dough is smooth and elastic and leaves your fingers and the sides of the bowl clean.
6. Lightly grease or oil the inside of a large polythene bag.
7. Slip the bowl of dough into the bag and leave in the ordinary warmth of the kitchen – not near direct heat or boiler – for 30 minutes to 1 hour, for the dough to rise. (The dough should double in size, so watch it during this time and don't leave it any longer than necessary.)
8. Remove from bag. Knead the caster sugar and salt into the risen dough.
9. Divide the dough into three equal parts. Roll each part into a fat sausage shape.
10. Seal the three sausage shapes together at one end. Plait them together then seal the other end.
11. Put the plait on a lightly greased baking sheet. Leave to prove (rise again) for about 15 minutes – the plait should look plump and swollen.
12. Preheat oven to hot, 220°C (425°F) or gas 7.
13. Bake the plait in the centre of the preheated oven for 30–35 minutes, or until bread is golden and sounds slightly hollow when tapped on the base.
14. Leave the plait to cool.
15. Mix the icing sugar with enough cold water to give a mixture which will thickly coat the back of a wooden spoon.
16. Spoon the icing on to the top of the plait. Decorate with halved glacé cherries.
17. Allow the icing to set before you serve the plait.

Serve tangy Marmalade loaf with △
morning coffee or afternoon tea.

If planning to freeze Cherry plait, ▷
do not ice until it has thawed and
is ready to eat.

LUXURY BUN ROUND

Serves about 6

225g (8oz) plain flour
25g (1oz) margarine
15g (½oz) fresh yeast
4 tablespoons tepid milk
4 tablespoons tepid water
1 small egg, beaten
large pinch of salt
40g (1½oz) caster sugar
25g (1oz) currants
150ml (¼ pint) double cream,
   whipped
2 heaped tablespoons
   strawberry jam
a little sifted icing sugar to
   decorate

1. Sift the flour into a bowl.
2. Rub in the margarine.
3. Cream the yeast with a little of
the tepid milk then add rest of
tepid liquids and egg.
4. Make a well in the flour, then
add yeast liquid and mix to a soft
dough.
5. Knead dough until smooth and
elastic.
6. Lightly grease or oil the inside
of a large polythene bag.
7. Slip the bowl of dough into the
bag.
8. Leave in a warm place – not
near direct heat or boiler – for
about 1½ hours, or until dough has
risen to twice its size.
9. Remove from bag. Knead salt
into risen dough with sugar and
currants.
10. Form mixture into two flat,
large rounds and put on to
greased baking sheet.
11. Leave in a warm place for 20
minutes.
12. Preheat oven to moderately
hot, 200°C (400°F) or gas 6.
13. Bake in centre of preheated
oven for 25–35 minutes or until
golden brown and cooked. Leave
to cool.
14. Sandwich rounds with cream
and jam; decorate top with icing
sugar, and serve the same day.

CHERRY CAKE

Serves about 6

225g (8oz) plain flour
2 level teaspoons baking
   powder
pinch of salt
175g (6oz) margarine
175g (6oz) caster sugar
3 medium eggs
75g (3oz) glacé cherries
1 tablespoon milk

1. Preheat oven to moderate,
180°C (350°F) or gas 4.
2. Line a deep 20cm (8 inch)
square cake tin with greaseproof
paper. Grease the paper.
3. Sift the flour with the baking
powder and salt.
4. Cream the margarine with the
sugar until light and fluffy.
5. Beat the eggs, then add them
very gradually to the creamed
mixture, beating all the time.
6. Wash the cherries in very hot
water; dry thoroughly. Cut each
cherry into four and toss them in
a little flour.
7. Fold flour and milk into the
creamed mixture.
8. Fold in the cherries so they are
evenly distributed.
9. Spoon mixture into prepared
tin and smooth top.
10. Bake in centre of preheated
oven for 1¾–2 hours, or until firm
to the touch.
11. Turn out to cool on a wire
cooling rack. This cake will keep
for a week if stored in an airtight
tin.

=== **COOK'S TIP** ===

Wash the cherries in hot water to
remove the syrup and stickiness.
This should allow the cherries to
stay evenly distributed throughout
the cake and not sink to the bottom.
As an alternative, replace the
cherries with 75g (3oz) chocolate
chips and 1 teaspoon vanilla
flavouring.

△ *Luxury bun round is always eaten
up quickly because of the tempting
aroma in the kitchen while it is
baking.*

◁ *Colourful cherry cake is a family
favourite.*

VICTORIA SANDWICH

Serves about 6

110g (4oz) margarine
110g (4oz) caster sugar, plus a
   little extra to sprinkle top of
   cooked cake
2 medium eggs
110g (4oz) self-raising flour,
   sifted
2 heaped tablespoons raspberry
   or strawberry jam

1. Preheat oven to moderately
hot, 190°C (375°F) or gas 5.
2. Grease two 18cm (7 inch) round
cake tins. Line bases of tins with
greaseproof paper and then grease
the paper.
3. Beat the margarine with 110g
(4oz) caster sugar until light and
fluffy.
4. Beat the eggs together then
beat into the mixture.
5. Using a metal spoon, fold in
the sifted flour.
6. Divide the mixture between the
cake tins.
7. Bake the cakes in the centre of
the preheated oven for 20–30
minutes, or until firm to the
touch.
8. Turn out to cool on a wire
rack.
9. Sandwich cakes with jam then
lightly dust top of cake with
caster sugar.

═══ COOK'S TIP ═══

This is a good basic recipe that can
be altered for different flavours.
Try adding the grated rind of 1
lemon with the creamed fat and
sugar, and 2 tablespoons lemon
juice with the flour. Sandwich
together with lemon curd. Or use
grated rind of 1 orange and 2
tablespoons juice in the mixture
and sandwich together with
apricot jam.

COFFEE GATEAU

Serves about 6

110g (4oz) plain flour
1½ level teaspoons baking
   powder
175g (6oz) margarine
110g (4oz) caster sugar
2 large eggs
1 level dessertspoon, plus 1
   level teaspoon instant coffee
   powder
100g (4oz) icing sugar
2 tablespoons raspberry,
   strawberry or plum jam

1. Preheat oven to moderately
hot, 190°C (375°F) or gas 5.
2. Grease two 18cm (7 inch) round
sandwich tins. Line with
greaseproof paper.
3. Sift the flour and baking
powder.
4. Cream 110g (4oz) margarine
with the caster sugar.
5. Add the eggs, one at a time,
beating well after each addition.
6. Fold in the flour using a metal
spoon.
7. Mix the dessertspoon of coffee
with a dessertspoon of boiling
water. Beat into the cake mixture.
8. Divide the mixture between the
prepared cake tins. Smooth the
tops.
9. Bake in the centre of the
preheated oven for 20–25 minutes
or until golden and firm.
10. Turn out cakes to cool on a
wire rack.
11. Sift the icing sugar.
12. Cream rest of margarine with
icing sugar and the teaspoon of
coffee until light and fluffy.
13. When the cakes are cool,
sandwich them together with the
jam.
14. Spread a little icing on top
and round the sides of the cake
and make a stippled pattern with
a fork.
15. Put the rest of the icing in a
piping bag with a medium-sized
star nozzle. Pipe lattice pattern
across the top of the cake, and
stars round edge and base.

*Versatile Victoria sandwich is △
quick to make, can be baked in any
shape of tin and be flavoured with
orange, lemon, coffee or chocolate.*

*Serve Coffee gâteau at a ▷
special tea party.*

WALNUT FUDGE CAKE

Serves 8–10

175g (6oz) soft margarine
175g (6oz) light soft brown
  sugar
3 large eggs
175g (6oz) self-raising flour
pinch of salt
50g (2oz) walnuts, chopped
2 tablespoons milk

Filling and decoration:
175g (6oz) margarine
2 tablespoons milk
1 level tablespoon malted milk
  powder or drinking chocolate
  powder
350g (12oz) icing sugar, sifted
50g (2oz) walnuts, chopped

1. Preheat oven to moderately
hot, 190°C (375°F) or gas 5.
2. Grease two 19cm (7½ inch)
sandwich tins with melted fat and
line the base of each with a circle
of greaseproof paper.
3. Put the margarine, sugar, eggs,
flour, salt, walnuts and milk into
a bowl.
4. Using a wooden spoon mix all
the ingredients together then beat
them for a minute.
5. Divide the mixture between the
two tins and level the surface.
6. Bake in the centre of the oven
for 25–30 minutes, until the cakes
feel springy to the touch and they
are coming away from the sides of
the tin.
7. Leave on a wire tray to cool
and remove the greaseproof paper.
8. Melt the margarine for the
filling, then remove the pan from
the heat and add the milk and the
malted milk or chocolate powder.
9. Gradually beat in the sifted
icing sugar and when it has all
been added and the icing is
smooth, leave it on one side to
cool and thicken.
10. Sandwich the two cakes
together with half the icing.
11. Spread the remainder on top
letting it flow down the sides of
the cake slightly.
12. Sprinkle the chopped walnuts
on the top for decoration.

SAINT CLEMENT'S CAKE

Serves about 6

110g (4oz) self-raising flour
50g (2oz) margarine
4 medium eggs
110g (4oz) caster sugar
2 level tablespoons lemon curd
275g (10oz) icing sugar
strained juice of half a medium
  lemon
few slices of orange and lemon
  crystallized sweets

1. Preheat oven to moderate,
180°C (350°F) or gas 4.
2. Grease a 20cm (8 inch) round,
deep cake tin. Line base of tin
with greaseproof paper.
3. Sift the flour into a bowl.
4. Melt the margarine in a small
pan. Leave to cool.
5. Put the eggs and the caster
sugar in a large bowl and whisk
until very pale and creamy. The
mixture should hold the
impression of the whisk for
5 seconds.
6. Fold the flour and melted
margarine into whisked mixture.
7. Pour into prepared cake tin
and bake in the centre of the
preheated oven for 30 minutes, or
until firm to the touch.
8. Turn out cake to cool on a wire
rack.
9. Cut the cake into three layers.
10. Sandwich the cake with the
lemon curd.
11. Sift icing sugar.
12. Mix lemon juice and a little
water into the icing sugar to
make an icing stiff enough to coat
the back of a wooden spoon.
13. Pour icing over cake so that
top and sides are coated. (Never
try to spread glacé icing.) Leave
to set.
14. Cut the orange and lemon
slices into strips and use to
decorate top of cake.

===== COOK'S TIP =====

Water or glacé icing must be mixed
swiftly and poured over the cake
quickly. However, do take time to
make sure the icing is the correct
consistency. Add the liquid slowly.
Always have 2 or 3 tablespoons
extra icing sugar to use if icing is
too runny. Leave the cake on a wire
cooling tray while icing so that it
can drip. Place cake on a plate
when the icing is dry.

△ *Rich Walnut fudge cake is topped
with a delicious icing and then
sprinkled with chopped walnuts.*

◁ *Eye-catching to look at, Saint
Clement's cake is really quite
simple to decorate.*

FORT CAKE

Cake:
175g (6oz) softened margarine
175g (6oz) caster sugar
3 large eggs
150g (5oz) self-raising flour
25g (1oz) cocoa powder
1 tablespoon milk

Icing:
175g (6oz) margarine, softened
200g (7oz) icing sugar, sifted
40g (1½oz) cocoa powder

Decoration:
little brown and green food
    colouring
25g (1oz) desiccated coconut
31 small chocolate flakes
10cm (4 inch) square piece plain
    chocolate

1. Preheat oven to moderately hot, 190°C (375°F) or gas 5.
2. Brush an 18cm (7 inch) square cake tin with melted fat and line the base with a piece of greaseproof paper cut to fit. Brush the paper lining.
3. For the cake, beat the margarine, sugar, eggs, sifted flour and cocoa powder together with the milk to make a soft dropping consistency.
4. Turn the mixture into the tin, spread it level then slightly hollow out the centre so the cake rises evenly during cooking.
5. Bake in the centre of the oven for 35–40 minutes, until it starts to shrink away from the sides of the tin and the cake feels springy to the touch.
6. Cool on a wire tray then remove the paper.
7. Beat the margarine for the icing, then gradually beat in the icing sugar and cocoa powder.
8. Work a little brown and green colouring into the coconut to make it look like grass.
9. Spread a 28cm (11 inch) cake board with a thin layer of icing then sprinkle over the coloured coconut.
10. Leaving a 4cm (1½ inch) border, cut the centre from the cake then cut this piece into nine small squares.
11. Spread the frame of the cake, now a hollow square, on the top, inside and outside with icing. Lift carefully and centre on the board.

12. Spread eight small pieces of cake with icing (the ninth one is spare) and place on top of main cake, one at each corner and one in the centre of each wall, to make eight turrets.
13. Along three of the walls position the flakes, sticking them to the walls in the order of two whole flakes and two halves, ending with two whole flakes. This should work out so that the whole flakes cover the turrets.
14. The fourth side is for the door. Cover the sides in the same way but leave the centre turret. To this stick the piece of plain chocolate and then stick a flake across the top for the cross beam.
15. Finally arrange model soldiers and Red Indians around the cake so the fort is under attack.

CHOCOLATE LOG CAKE

Serves about 6

175g (6oz) butter
350g (12oz) icing sugar
40g (1½oz) cocoa powder
1 medium egg
chocolate Swiss roll
little sifted icing sugar to
    decorate

1. Beat the butter until it is light and fluffy.
2. Sift the icing sugar and cocoa together and beat them into the butter with the egg.
3. Spread the buttercream over the roll, marking it with a knife to give the appearance of bark. Sprinkle with sifted icing sugar.
4. For a festive touch, decorate the serving board or dish with a sprig of holly.

=== **COOK'S TIP** ===

Choose a large Swiss roll for this log. If making your own cake, use a 3-egg mixture. A most attractive cake to look at, it has the advantage of disguising any small cracks that sometimes appear when rolling up the cake.

For a boy's birthday cake, nothing △ would be as popular as a chocolate Fort cake.

Serve Chocolate log cake at a ▷ Christmas party or at any other time of year.

ITALIAN TORRONE

Makes 12–16 slices

110g (4oz) soft margarine
75g (3oz) cocoa powder
150g (5oz) ground almonds
1 egg
110g (4oz) caster sugar
2 tablespoons water
50g (2oz) semi-sweet biscuits
25g (1oz) glacé cherries,
   chopped
25g (1oz) walnuts, chopped
walnut halves and 2 glacé
   cherries to decorate

1. Mix margarine and cocoa
powder together until soft.
2. Add ground almonds and egg,
mix in well.
3. Place sugar and water in a
saucepan and dissolve gently.
4. Pour on to cocoa mixture and
beat well.
5. Break biscuits into almond-size
pieces and add to the mixture,
together with cherries and
walnuts.
6. Place in a 20cm (8 inch)
sandwich tin lined with
greaseproof paper; smooth top
with a knife and leave to set in a
refrigerator or cold place.
7. Ease around the edge with a
knife and turn out on to a plate.
8. Decorate with walnuts and
glacé cherries and serve
immediately, or return to
refrigerator until required.

═══ COOK'S TIP ═══

Delicious, rich and uncooked, this
recipe is quick to prepare. You may
prefer to put it in a square 18 cm
(7 inch) tin and cut the torrone into
bite sized pieces to serve at coffee
time. Digestive biscuits crumble
well for the filling.

BOTERLETTER

Serves 4–6

Pastry:
225g (8oz) plain flour
175g (6oz) butter
scant 125ml (¼ pint) water

Almond paste:
175g (6oz) ground almonds
175g (6oz) caster sugar
1 egg
juice of half a lemon
almond essence
beaten egg to glaze
15g (½oz) angelica, 2 glacé
   cherries to decorate

1. Preheat oven to hot, 220°C
(425°F) or gas 7.
2. Make pastry with flour, butter
and water. Roll into a long strip
approximately 10cm (4 inches)
wide and 3mm (⅛ inch) thick.
3. Mix almond paste ingredients
together and form into a long
sausage shape, using your hands,
and making it just a little shorter
than the length of pastry. Place
on top of the pastry strip. Wrap
pastry around the paste, sealing
the edge and ends with beaten
egg. Place on a baking sheet and
form into the shape of a letter.
4. Glaze with beaten egg. Bake in
the centre of the oven for
approximately 30 minutes.
5. When golden brown, remove
from the oven and allow to cool.
Decorate with chopped angelica
and glacé cherries and serve, cut
in slices, with tea or coffee.

△ *Italian torrone is a chocolate cake
which is set in the refrigerator as it
needs no cooking.*

◁ *Boterletter is a filling pastry cake
containing almond paste. It is
always shaped into a letter.*

CHELSEA BUNS

Makes 12

225g (8oz) plain flour
65g (2½oz) margarine
15g (½oz) fresh yeast
6 tablespoons tepid milk
1 small egg, beaten
pinch of salt
90g (3½oz) caster sugar
25g (1oz) sultanas
25g (1oz) currants
25g (1oz) chopped mixed peel

1. Sift the flour into a mixing bowl.
2. Rub in 40g (1½oz) margarine until mixture resembles fine breadcrumbs.
3. Cream the fresh yeast with a little of the tepid milk then stir in the rest of the milk and the beaten egg.
4. Make a well in the centre of the flour. Add the yeast liquid and beat well.
5. Knead for at least 5 minutes until the dough is smooth and elastic and leaves your fingers and the sides of the bowl clean.
6. Lightly grease or oil the inside of a large polythene bag.
7. Slip the bowl of dough inside the bag and leave in a warm place – not near direct heat or boiler – for 45 minutes, or until dough has doubled in size.
8. Remove from bag. Turn dough on to lightly floured board and knead in the salt and 15g (½oz) sugar.
9. Roll out the dough to an oblong 30cm (12 inches) by 23cm (9 inches).
10. Melt the rest of the margarine in a small pan and stir in the sultanas, currants and peel.
11. Spread the fruit evenly over the dough, leaving a 2.5cm (1 inch) space all round the edge.
12. Brush one long edge with water. Starting at the other long edge, roll up dough tightly and press all the edges to seal.
13. Cut the dough roll into 12 slices.
14. Grease a meat tin.
15. Arrange the dough slices in the tin, leaving about 1cm (½ inch) space between each slice. (They will join up as they cook.)
16. Flatten the buns slightly and leave to prove (rise again) for 15 minutes.
17. Preheat oven to hot, 220°C (425°F) or gas 7.
18. Bake the buns in the centre of the preheated oven for 20 minutes, or until golden.
19. Take buns out of oven and pull them apart.
20. Sprinkle rest of sugar over the buns and leave to cool. Eat them the same day.

ICED BUN TWISTS

Makes 8

225g (8oz) plain flour
25g (1oz) margarine
15g (½oz) fresh yeast
4 tablespoons tepid milk
4 tablespoons tepid water
1 small egg, beaten
large pinch salt
40g (1½oz) caster sugar
25g (1oz) currants
75g (3oz) icing sugar

1. Sift the flour into a bowl.
2. Rub in the margarine.
3. Cream the fresh yeast with a little of the tepid milk then add rest of tepid liquids and egg.
4. Make a well in the flour, then add yeast liquid and mix to a soft dough.
5. Knead dough until smooth and elastic.
6. Lightly grease or oil the inside of a large polythene bag.
7. Slip bowl of dough into the bag.
8. Leave in a warm place – not near direct heat or boiler – for about 1½ hours, or until dough has risen to twice its size.
9. Remove from bag. Knead in salt, sugar and currants.
10. Form mixture into eight, then divide each piece into three. Make into three short fat sausage shapes. Twist lightly together then form into a round shape. Repeat with rest of dough.
11. Leave, on a greased baking sheet, in warm place for 20 minutes.
12. Preheat oven to moderately hot, 200°C (400°F) or gas 6.
13. Bake in centre of preheated oven for 20–25 minutes, or until golden and cooked.
14. Leave to cool.
15. Sift icing sugar and add enough cold water to give thick mixture which will coat back of wooden spoon. Spoon on to top of each bun. Leave to set, and eat the same day.

═══ COOK'S TIP ═══

Fresh yeast can usually be bought from your local baker, and it also comes in tins. The small, putty-coloured granules need longer to start working but are just as good if directions on the can are followed closely.

There is nothing quite like home- △ made Chelsea buns, a little time-consuming to make but worth it.

For a mid morning snack or at ▷ teatime, make and serve Iced bun twists.

RING DOUGHNUTS

Makes 12

**225g (8oz) plain flour
pinch of salt
2 level teaspoons baking
  powder
50g (2oz) margarine
65g (2½oz) caster sugar
1 medium egg, beaten
milk to mix
clean lard or corn oil for deep
  frying**

1. Sift the flour with the salt and baking powder into a mixing bowl.
2. Rub margarine into flour until mixture resembles fine breadcrumbs.
3. Mix in 50g (2oz) sugar.
4. Beat in the egg and enough milk to give a fairly soft, but not sticky, consistency.
5. Turn dough on to lightly floured board and knead gently until smooth.
6. Roll out the dough to 1cm (½ inch) thickness.
7. Using a plain 5cm (2 inch) cutter, cut out nine rounds. Using a much smaller cutter or a knife, cut out the centre of the rounds to make rings. Re-roll centres and make more rings.
8. Fry the doughnuts in a deep pan of hot fat or oil for 5–7 minutes, or until golden brown and crisp.
9. Drain doughnuts on soft kitchen paper and toss them in rest of sugar. Eat the same day, hot or cold.

SCOTCH PANCAKES

Makes 12

**110g (4oz) self-raising flour
1 level teaspoon baking powder
½ level teaspoon salt
1 egg
2 tablespoons cooking oil
150ml (¼ pint) milk
oil for cooking**

1. Sift flour, baking powder and salt in a bowl. Make a well in centre. ·
2. Beat egg and blend in oil and milk. Add to centre of flour. Gradually mix in flour and beat well.
3. Heat a large frying pan and grease lightly with oil. Put tablespoons of batter in pan well apart. Cook till full of bubbles on top and golden brown underneath. Turn and cook underside.

=== **COOK'S TIP** ===

The American way of serving pancakes for breakfast, lunch or brunch is becoming increasingly popular.

Try pancakes with scrambled eggs, eggs and bacon, sliced liver, kidneys or sausages as savouries.

Pancakes with golden syrup, honey, jams or jellies make a sweet treat at any time of the day.

Pancakes are good eaten straight from the pan, so if you have several mouths to feed make larger pancakes, the size of the pan, put on serving plate and top with soft fruit and ice cream.

△ *The dough for Ring doughnuts can be made the day before and kept in the refrigerator, well wrapped, ready to fry.*

◁ *Familiar Scotch pancakes can be served with sweet and savoury toppings.*

CANDLE CUP CAKES

Makes 12

110g (4oz) plain flour
1 level teaspoon baking powder
pinch of salt
75g (3oz) margarine
75g (3oz) caster sugar
1 large egg, beaten
1 tablespoon orange squash,
    undiluted
100g (4oz) icing sugar
pink food colouring
12 tiny birthday candles in
    holders

1. Preheat oven to moderately hot, 190°C (375°F) or gas 5.
2. Line 12 bun tins with paper cases.
3. Sift the flour with the baking powder and salt.
4. Cream the margarine with the caster sugar until light and fluffy.
5. Add beaten egg to creamed mixture a little at a time.
6. Stir in the orange squash.
7. Fold in the flour.
8. Spoon mixture into cake cases.
9. Bake in the centre of the preheated oven for 15 minutes. Leave to cool in their paper cases.
10. Mix icing sugar with enough cold water to make an icing which will thickly coat the back of a wooden spoon.
11. Colour the icing a delicate pink, dropping colour from top of skewer or knitting needle.
12. Spoon icing on to cakes.
13. While the icing is still wet, add a tiny candle in its holder to centre of each cake. Leave to set.

BUTTERFLIES

Makes 12

110g (4oz) plain flour
1 level teaspoon baking powder
pinch of salt
150g (5oz) margarine
75g (3oz) caster sugar
1 large egg, beaten
100g (4oz) icing sugar, sifted

1. Preheat oven to moderately hot, 190°C (375°F) or gas 5.
2. Line 12 bun tins with paper cake cases.
3. Sift the flour with the baking powder and salt.
4. Cream 75g (3oz) margarine with the caster sugar until light and fluffy.
5. Add beaten egg a little at a time, beating well.
6. Using a metal spoon, fold in the flour.
7. Spoon the mixture into the cake cases.
8. Bake in the centre of the preheated oven for 15 minutes, or until golden and firm to the touch.
9. Leave buns to cool in paper cases.
10. Beat the rest of the margarine with the icing sugar until light and very creamy.
11. Cut top off each bun. Cut each top in half to make two semi-circles.
12. Pipe or spoon the icing on top of each bun.
13. Place two semi-circles on top of each bun, at an angle and with the straight sides outwards, so they look like butterfly wings.

=== **COOK'S TIP** ===

For further decoration, cut two thin pieces of angelica about 2.5cm (1 inch) long and put in at one end of each butterfly for feelers. Three or four small silver balls down the centre will decorate the body even more.

To make baskets instead of butterflies cut a long, thin strip of angelica to go from one end of the cake to the other in a loop. Put coloured balls round sides of the cake to look like flowers peeping out.

Candle cup cakes are an △ inexpensive and pretty idea for a children's party, when there is no time to decorate a large cake.

Novelty Butterflies are for ▷ children's parties, too.

APPLE SQUARES

Makes 9

1 large cooking apple
25g (1oz) granulated sugar
110g (4oz) self-raising flour
110g (4oz) margarine
110g (4oz) caster sugar
2 medium eggs
milk to mix
150ml (¼ pint) whipping cream
150ml (¼ pint) cold, thick
   custard
1 large red eating apple

1. Preheat oven to moderately
hot, 190°C (375°F) or gas 5.
2. Grease a 20cm (8 inch) square,
fairly deep cake tin. Line tin with
greaseproof paper. Grease the
paper.
3. Peel, core and slice the cooking
apple and stew with granulated
sugar and one tablespoon water.
Drain well and leave to cool.
4. Sift the flour.
5. Cream the margarine with the
caster sugar until light and fluffy.
6. Add the beaten eggs a little at
a time and beating well.
7. Using a metal spoon, carefully
fold in the flour.
8. Add enough milk to give a
consistency which will drop easily
from a spoon when shaken.
9. Spoon mixture into prepared
tin and bake in centre of the
preheated oven for 30–45 minutes,
or until golden brown and firm to
the touch.
10. Leave the cake to cool on
wire rack.
11. Whip the cream until thick,
mix half with the cold custard and
stewed apple, reserving half for
topping.
12. Cut the cake into nine equal
pieces. Cut each piece into two
layers and sandwich them with
cream mixture.
13. Wash and core the red apple
but don't peel it. Cut it into
wedges.
14. Spread the rest of the cream
on top of the cakes. Decorate with
apple wedges and serve
immediately. (If you can't serve
the cakes at once, dip the apple
slices in lemon juice to prevent
them from discolouring.)

CHOCOLATE TRUFFLES

*Makes 18 large cakes or 36–40
small sweets*

450g (1lb) cake crumbs
225g (8oz) icing sugar, sifted
110g (4oz) cocoa powder
150ml (¼ pint) milk
1 dessertspoon rum
chocolate strands

1. Put the cake crumbs into a
bowl and mix in the sifted icing
sugar.
2. Sift in the cocoa powder.
3. Bind the ingredients together
with the milk and rum to make a
fairly stiff mixture.
4. Divide it into 18 even-sized,
large pieces or 36–40 small pieces
and roll them in your hands to
make balls.
5. Place the chocolate strands in
a polythene bag.
6. Add the balls two at a time and
shake the bag so the balls are well
coated with the strands.
7. Place each chocolate truffle in
a paper case or sweet case for
serving.

=== COOK'S TIP ===

This mixture may be made in a
mixer, when all the ingredients are
placed in the bowl and the machine
is switched on low until they are
combined.
  A plain, stale madeira cake
would be ideal for these truffles.
Stand a grater in a mixing bowl and
rub the cake against the largest
grating side to break up the cake.
Fruit, plain sponge or chocolate
cake could also be used. Fruit cake
would not be easy to crumble, so
cut it into small pieces.

△ *Spongy Apple squares are
sandwiched with a cream, custard
and apple mixture and then topped
with cream.*

◁ *Rich Chocolate truffles, flavoured
with rum, can be made large as
cakes or tiny as sweetmeats.*

LEMON SCONES

Makes 7

225g (8oz) self-raising flour
large pinch of salt
75g (3oz) margarine
25g (1oz) caster sugar
1 medium egg, beaten
milk to mix
3 heaped tablespoons lemon curd
50g (2oz) icing sugar, sifted
crystallized lemon slices

1. Preheat oven to hot, 230°C (450°F) or gas 8.
2. Lightly grease a baking sheet.
3. Sift the flour with the salt into a bowl.
4. Rub in 50g (2oz) of the margarine.
5. Stir in the caster sugar with the beaten egg and enough milk to give a soft, light dough.
6. Roll out the dough to about 1cm ($\frac{1}{2}$ inch) thickness.
7. Using a plain 5cm (2 inch) cutter, cut out seven rounds.
8. Put the scones on the prepared baking sheet and cook in oven for 10–15 minutes, or until golden.
9. Leave scones to cool on wire rack.
10. Split the scones then sandwich with 2 tablespoons of the lemon curd.
11. Beat the rest of the lemon curd with the remaining margarine and the icing sugar until fluffy.
12. Spread this mixture on top of each scone.
13. Cut crystallized lemon slices into small pieces and use to decorate the top of each scone. Serve the same day.

CORNISH SCONES

Makes 7

225g (8oz) self-raising flour
large pinch of salt
50g (2oz) margarine
25g (1oz) caster sugar
1 medium egg, beaten
milk to mix
1 carton Cornish clotted cream or 150ml ($\frac{1}{4}$ pint) double cream, whipped
strawberry jam

1. Preheat oven to hot, 230°C (450°F) or gas 8.
2. Lightly grease a baking sheet.
3. Sift the flour with the salt into a bowl.
4. Rub in the margarine.
5. Stir in sugar.
6. Add egg and enough milk to give soft, light dough.
7. Roll out to at least 1cm ($\frac{1}{2}$ inch) thickness.
8. Using a large plain pastry cutter, cut out seven rounds.
9. Bake in centre of preheated oven for 10–15 minutes, or until golden and firm.
10. Leave to cool.
11. Serve with jam and stiffly whipped cream.

===== COOK'S TIP =====

Strawberry jam is traditional but other jams such as blackcurrant and damson have distinctive flavours. It is not necessary to butter the scones when serving cream, but when using this recipe for a plain afternoon tea scone, butter and serve with jam or clear honey.

For other flavourings, add 50g (2oz) dried fruit or 50g (2oz) finely grated Cheddar cheese to the plain scone mixture.

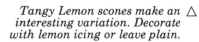
Tangy Lemon scones make an △ interesting variation. Decorate with lemon icing or leave plain.

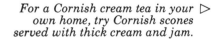
For a Cornish cream tea in your ▷ own home, try Cornish scones served with thick cream and jam.

CHOCOLATE TOPS

Makes 14

450g (1lb) self-raising flour
1 level teaspoon salt
110g (4oz) margarine
50g (2oz) caster sugar
2 medium eggs, beaten
milk to mix
175g (6oz) plain chocolate
strawberry jam (optional)

1. Preheat oven to hot, 230°C (450°F) or gas 8.
2. Lightly grease two baking sheets.
3. Sift the flour with the salt into a bowl.
4. Rub in the margarine.
5. Stir in the sugar.
6. Add the beaten eggs and just enough milk to mix to a soft, light dough.
7. Roll out the dough to at least 1cm (½ inch) thickness.
8. Using a plain 5cm (2 inch) pastry cutter, cut out 14 rounds.
9. Put the rounds on the prepared baking sheets and bake in centre of preheated oven for 10–15 minutes or until golden.
10. Leave the scones to cool on a wire rack.
11. Melt the chocolate in a basin over a pan of gently simmering water.
12. Dip the top of each scone in melted chocolate to coat. Leave to become hard and set.
13. Split the scones in half and sandwich with strawberry jam, if wished. Serve within 3 hours of adding the chocolate.

═══ COOK'S TIP ═══

Cooking chocolate comes in plain or milk chocolate bars and directions for use are on the packet. Confectionery chocolate can be used in some cooking but take care not to melt over direct heat. Use a bowl standing over hot, not boiling, water and do not keep the chocolate waiting long or it will dry dull.

GINGER SCONES

Makes 7

225g (8oz) self-raising flour
large pinch of salt
1 level teaspoon powdered
** ginger**
50g (2oz) margarine
25g (1oz) caster sugar
1 medium egg, beaten
milk to mix
150ml (¼ pint) double cream,
** whipped**
2 or 3 lumps crystallized ginger
** or stem ginger**

1. Preheat oven to hot, 230°C (450°F) or gas 8.
2. Lightly grease a baking sheet.
3. Sift the flour with salt and powdered ginger into a bowl. Do this twice.
4. Rub in the margarine.
5. Stir in the sugar.
6. Add the beaten egg and just enough milk to mix to a soft, light dough.
7. Roll out the dough to at least 1cm (½ inch) thickness.
8. Using a 5cm (2 inch) plain cutter, cut out seven rounds.
9. Put the rounds on the baking sheet and bake in centre of preheated oven for 10–15 minutes, or until golden.
10. Leave scones to cool on wire rack.
11. Split the scones in half.
12. Whip the cream slightly.
13. Chop the ginger and stir it into the cream.
14. Sandwich scones with the ginger cream and eat the same day.

△ *For a gathering of children, serve Chocolate tops sandwiched with strawberry jam.*

◁ *Filled with ginger cream, Ginger scones are easy to make and impressive to serve.*

MARMALADE SCONES

Makes 7

225g (8oz) self-raising flour
large pinch of salt
50g (2oz) margarine
25g (1oz) caster sugar
1 medium egg, beaten
milk to mix
4 heaped tablespoons rough-
    cut marmalade
rind of 1 small orange

1. Preheat oven to hot, 230°C
(450°F) or gas 8.
2. Lightly grease a baking sheet.
3. Sift the flour with the salt into
a large bowl.
4. Rub in the margarine.
5. Stir in the sugar.
6. Add the beaten egg and enough
milk to mix to a soft, light dough.
7. Roll out dough to at least 1cm
(½ inch) thickness.
8. Using a plain 5cm (2 inch)
cutter, cut out seven rounds.
9. Put the rounds on a baking
sheet and bake in centre of
preheated oven for 10–15 minutes,
or until golden.
10. Leave to cool on a wire rack.
11. Split the scones, and
sandwich them with a little of the
marmalade.
12. Remove the soft white pith
from the orange rind. Using a
sharp knife, cut the rind into fine
shreds.
13. Put the rind in a pan, add
water and boil for 3 minutes. Drain
and rinse in cold water then drain
again. Leave to cool.
14. Spread the rest of the
marmalade on the top of the
scones.
15. Sprinkle orange rind on top of
marmalade and serve that day.

=== COOK'S TIP ===

If short of time, buy one of the jelly
marmalades that have fine shreds
of peel throughout and use as a
topping in place of the orange peel.
Lemon marmalade would be
equally good.

CHOCOLATE ECLAIRS

Makes 12

150g (5oz) plain flour
pinch of salt
50g (2oz) margarine
3 medium eggs, beaten
300ml (½ pint) double cream,
    whipped
50g (2oz) icing sugar
1 level tablespoon cocoa

1. Preheat oven to hot, 220°C
(450°F) or gas 7.
2. Grease a large baking sheet.
3. Sift the flour and salt into a
bowl.
4. Put the margarine in a pan
with 300ml (½ pint) cold water.
Heat gently until the margarine
has melted but do not allow to
boil.
5. Using a wooden spoon, mix in
the flour. Beat well over a gentle
heat until mixture leaves sides of
pan.
6. Take off heat and allow to cool
slightly.
7. Very gradually, add the beaten
eggs to the mixture, beating all
the time.
8. When the mixture is very
smooth, put it in a piping bag
fitted with a 2cm (¾ inch) plain
nozzle.
9. Pipe 12 lines, each 13cm
(5 inches) long on two baking
sheets.
10. Bake in the centre of the
preheated oven for 30 minutes, or
until golden brown and fairly
crisp.
11. Cut each éclair in half and,
using a small spoon, carefully
scoop out any soft mixture.
12. Spoon cream into both the
hollowed-out halves and sandwich
together again.
13. Sift the icing sugar with the
cocoa. Add enough hot water to
make an icing which will coat the
back of a wooden spoon.
14. Spoon some icing on top of
each bun, or quickly dip the top
of each bun in icing. Leave to set
and eat the same day.

*Serve marmalade scones with △
morning coffee.*

*Once you have mastered the art of ▷
choux pastry, Chocolate éclairs
will become a simple to make treat
for any occasion.*

SPECIAL MINCE PIES

Makes 18–20

4 tablespoons water
220g (7oz) lard
250g (9oz) plain flour
40g (1½oz) cornflour
½ level teaspoon baking powder
pinch of salt
generous 225g (8oz) mincemeat
squeeze of lemon juice
icing sugar to sprinkle

1. Preheat oven to moderately hot, 200°C (400°F) or gas 6.
2. Put the water and lard into a fairly large pan and, over a low heat, melt the lard.
3. Sift the flour, cornflour, baking powder and salt together on to a piece of paper.
4. Shoot the dry ingredients into the liquid and stir well to form a soft dough.
5. Wrap the dough in foil or greaseproof paper and leave it in a cool place overnight.
6. Next day roll out the pastry and cut out an equal number of large and small rounds, using 6cm (2½ inch) and 5 cm (2 inch) cutters.
7. Line deep tartlet tins with the larger rounds. Mix the mincemeat with the lemon juice. Fill each round with 1 teaspoon of mincemeat
8. Moisten the pastry edges and put on the tops.
9. Using the rim of an upturned wine glass, press the two joined edges firmly together.
10. Make a hole in the centre of each pie with a skewer.
11. Bake in the centre of the oven for 35–40 minutes, until the pastry is light golden brown.
12. Dust the mince pies with icing sugar before serving hot or cold.

STRAWBERRY TARTLETS

Makes 12

150g (5oz) plain flour
pinch of salt
65g (2½oz) margarine
1 small egg yolk, beaten
2 heaped tablespoons strawberry jam, sieved
500g (1lb) fresh strawberries (when in season) or 1 large can strawberries
150ml (¼ pint) double cream

1. Preheat oven to hot, 220°C (425°F) or gas 7.
2. Lightly grease 12 patty tins.
3. Sift flour and salt into a bowl.
4. Rub in margarine.
5. Add enough egg yolk to give stiff dough.
6. Use to line prepared tins.
7. Bake blind (see page 7) in centre of preheated oven for 15–20 minutes. Remove paper and beans if used. Allow to cool.
8. Spoon jam into each tartlet and cover it with prepared or drained fruit.
9. Whip cream. Decorate with piped stars and eat the same day.

===== COOK'S TIP =====

Preserved strawberries do not have the same appearance or flavour as the fresh fruit. Strawberries frozen individually on a tray and then bagged would be good for these tarts, and fresh or frozen raspberries, too. If you would like to try fresh loganberries or blackberries then use raspberry jam.

△ *The shortcrust pastry used to make these Special mince pies is especially good. The dough will keep in the refrigerator for a week or more.*

◁ *Serve pretty Strawberry tartlets for a party or buffet spread.*

CREAM HORNS

Makes 6

puff pastry made with 110g
  (4oz) flour (see Basic recipes,
  page 7)
1 small egg yolk, beaten
2 heaped tablespoons raspberry
  or strawberry jam
150ml (¼ pint) double cream,
  whipped

1. Preheat oven to hot, 230°C
(450°F) or gas 8.
2. Wet a baking sheet but don't
grease it. Grease six cream horn
tins.
3. Roll out pastry into a thin,
neat oblong. Cut six neat strips
and wet these lightly.
4. Starting at pointed end of tin,
and overlapping pastry as you
work, wind pastry strip around
each tin. Seal with a little egg
yolk and brush rest over pastry.
5. Bake in centre of preheated
oven for 15–20 minutes or until
pale golden. Remove tins. Allow
to cool.
6. Fill first with jam, then cream
and eat within 2 hours.

===== COOK'S TIP =====

Cream horns are ideal for tea but
equally good with a savoury filling,
especially for a party or buffet
supper. Make 300 ml (½ pint) thick
white sauce (see Basic recipes,
page 6) and to this add 2
tablespoons thin cream or top of
the milk and 1 tablespoon sherry.
To this sauce add any one of the
following: 200g (7oz) can shrimps,
drained; 200g (7oz) can tuna,
drained and flaked; 175g (6oz)
cooked, chopped ham, or 175g (6oz)
cooked, chopped chicken. Serve on
a bed of lettuce and decorate with
slices of hard-boiled egg, cooked
button mushrooms or tomatoes.

COCONUT BISCUITS

Makes 10

110g (4oz) margarine
50g (2oz) caster sugar
1 medium egg
150g (5oz) plain flour, sifted
150g (5oz) desiccated coconut
2 tablespoons apricot jam
pink food colouring
5 glacé cherries

1. Preheat oven to moderately
hot, 190°C (375°F) or gas 5.
2. Grease a baking sheet.
3. Beat the margarine with the
sugar until mixture is light and
fluffy.
4. Add the egg and beat well.
5. Using a metal spoon, fold in
the flour and 50g (2oz) of the
desiccated coconut.
6. Lightly knead the mixture then
roll out very thinly.
7. Cut mixture into 10 rounds and
put on prepared baking sheet.
8. Bake in centre of preheated
oven for 15 minutes, or until
golden.
9. Leave biscuits to cool.
10. Warm jam, sieve it and brush
on tops of biscuits.
11. Mix a tiny amount of
colouring with 1 tablespoon
water. Stir this into the remaining
coconut to colour it a delicate
pink.
12. Put the coloured coconut on
the top of the biscuits.
13. Decorate each biscuit with
half a glacé cherry.

*Cream horns are teatime pastries △
that need to be eaten with a fork.
Do not fill too long before eating.*

*Coconut biscuits look attractive ▷
with their jam and coconut topping
and glacé cherry decoration.*

EASTER BONNETS

Makes 14

75g (3oz) margarine
75g (3oz) caster sugar
175g (6oz) plain flour
finely grated rind of 1 lemon
little beaten egg
50g (2oz) butter
50g (2oz) icing sugar, sifted
little coffee essence
crystallized violets and mimosa

1. Preheat oven to moderately hot, 200°C (400°F) or gas 6.
2. Beat the margarine and sugar together until soft and fluffy.
3. Mix in the flour and grated lemon rind with enough beaten egg to make a dough of shortcrust pastry consistency.
4. On a lightly floured working surface roll the dough out to just under a 3mm ($\frac{1}{8}$ inch) thickness.
5. Cut out an even number of large and small rounds using 6cm (2$\frac{1}{2}$ inch) and 3cm (1$\frac{1}{4}$ inch) fluted cutters.
6. Gather up the scraps and cut out more rounds.
7. Place the biscuits on a baking sheet and cook in the centre of the oven for about 8 minutes. (The smaller ones will be ready first.) Cool on a wire tray.
8. Beat the butter to a soft cream, then gradually beat in the icing sugar with enough coffee essence to flavour and colour.
9. Place the filling in a piping bag with a star pipe attached.
10. Pipe a swirl just slightly off centre of the larger biscuits.
11. Top with a small biscuit to make the crown of the bonnet.
12. Decorate with crystallized violets and mimosa for trimmings.

===== COOK'S TIP =====

If you are having a party, repeat the recipe using 2 level tablespoons cocoa in the biscuit mixture. This will need a little more egg to mix. Try using other sizes of cutters as well. When putting bonnets together, mix and match the chocolate and plain brims and crowns for greater variety.

GINGERBREAD MEN

Makes 12

150g (5oz) plain flour
pinch of salt
$\frac{1}{2}$ level teaspoon ground ginger
$\frac{1}{4}$ level teaspoon bicarbonate of soda
1$\frac{1}{4}$ tablespoons golden syrup
15g ($\frac{1}{2}$oz) caster sugar
25g (1oz) margarine
half a medium egg, beaten
currants, angelica, glacé cherries and silver balls to decorate

1. Preheat oven to moderate, 180°C (350°F) or gas 4.
2. Lightly grease two large baking sheets.
3. Sift the flour with the salt, ginger and bicarbonate of soda.
4. Put the syrup, caster sugar and margarine in a pan and melt them over a gentle heat.
5. Cool slightly then stir into flour mixture.
6. Add enough of the egg to mix to a stiff dough.
7. Roll out dough thinly.
8. Cut into gingerbread men shapes with cutter or cut round cardboard shape with a knife.
9. Put the men on the prepared baking sheets. Give each a pair of currant eyes, an angelica smiling, upturned mouth and silver balls or chopped glacé cherries for buttons.
10. Bake in centre of preheated oven for 7–10 minutes, or until golden and firm to touch. Leave to cool. (These keep well if stored in an airtight tin.)

△ *For a tea party to remember, serve Easter bonnets, colourfully decorated with violets and mimosa.*

◁ *If you have no Gingerbread men cutter, make a shape out of cardboard and cut round this.*

JAM CIRCLES

Makes 15

200g (7oz) plain flour
large pinch of salt
150g (5oz) margarine
110g (4oz) caster sugar
1 medium egg, beaten
40g (1½oz) icing sugar
3 heaped tablespoons rasberry jam

1. Preheat oven to moderately hot, 190°C (375°F) or gas 5.
2. Grease two baking sheets.
3. Sift flour and salt into a bowl.
4. Rub in margarine until the mixture resembles fine breadcrumbs.
5. Stir in the caster sugar.
6. Add the beaten egg and work lightly to a firm dough.
7. Roll out thinly.
8. Using a 6cm (2½ inch) fluted cutter, cut out 15 rounds.
9. Remove centre of each round with a smaller cutter. Re-roll centres and cut out 15 rounds. do not remove the centres from these.
10. Put all the biscuits on the prepared baking sheets and bake in centre of preheated oven for 15 minutes or until golden.
11. Cool the biscuits.
12. Sift the icing sugar and sprinkle it on the biscuit rings.
13. Sandwich biscuits in pairs with the rings on top using a little of the jam. Carefully spoon or pipe the rest of the jam into the centre of each biscuit sandwich.
14. Store in an airtight tin and eat within three days.

═══ COOK'S TIP ═══

For a children's party, vary this recipe by making traffic lights. Cut out three small circles instead of one and fill with raspberry and apricot jam and lemon curd with green food colouring. The biscuits can be stored longer if not filled.

CREAM OAT CRISPS

Makes 6

110g (4oz) granulated sugar
25g (1oz) margarine
1 medium egg
75g (3oz) oatmeal (not the instant kind)
½ level teaspoon baking powder
pinch of salt
vanilla essence to taste
150ml (¼ pint) double cream

1. Preheat oven to moderately hot, 190°C (375°F) or gas 5.
2. Grease two large baking sheets.
3. Cream the sugar with the margarine until light and fluffy.
4. Add the egg, beating well.
5. Mix the oatmeal with the baking powder and salt. Stir into mixture.
6. Add vanilla essence to taste.
7. Drop mixture in heaped teaspoonfuls on to prepared baking sheets. Space very well apart.
8. Bake in centre of preheated oven for 10 minutes, or until firm to touch.
9. Leave to cool on baking sheets for 2 minutes then turn out to complete cooling on a wire rack.
10. Whip cream slightly and use to sandwich the biscuits together. Serve immediately.

═══ COOK'S TIP ═══

Use oatmeal or rolled oats that need cooking for this recipe. If you cannot find oatmeal in the supermarket, try a health food shop. Oatmeal takes a long time to cook for porridge but can be used in place of ¼ of the flour in gingerbread. Try using it for coating fish instead of crumbs before frying.

Home-made biscuits are always △ welcome, try novel Jam circles filled with your favourite jam.

Crunchy Cream oat crisps are ▷ sandwiched with lightly whipped cream – popular with teenagers.

CHOCOLATE OAT BISCUITS

Makes 14

175g (6oz) margarine
150g (5oz) demerara or raw
  sugar
1 tablespoon golden syrup
225g (8oz) oatmeal (not the
  instant kind)
large pinch of salt
75g (3oz) milk or plain
  chocolate

1. Preheat oven to moderately
hot, 190°C (375°F) or gas 5.
2. Grease an oblong baking tin
about 28cm (11 inches) by 18cm
(7 inches).
3. Put the margarine in a pan and
melt it over a gentle heat.
4. Stir the sugar into the
margarine with the syrup,
oatmeal and salt. Stir well.
5. Put mixture in prepared tin;
smooth the top and bake in centre
of preheated oven for 30 minutes,
or until golden.
6. Bring out of oven, mark 14
neat oblongs with a knife and
leave to cool in the tin.
7. Melt the chocolate in a basin
over a pan of gently simmering
water.
8. Cut the cooled mixture into 14
oblongs.
9. Dip half of each oblong into
the liquid chocolate. Leave to
become hard and set. Eat the
same day.

=== COOK'S TIP ===

See Cook's Tip on previous page
about oatmeal. After dipping the
oblongs in chocolate, leave to cool
on a wire tray or piece of waxed
paper. Chocolate does not stick to
waxed paper.

CHOCOLATE FANCIES

Makes 26

275g (10oz) plain flour
large pinch of salt
75g (3oz) caster sugar
175g (6oz) margarine
vanilla essence, to taste
15g (½oz) cocoa

1. Preheat oven to moderate,
180°C (350°F) or gas 4.
2. Lightly grease two baking
sheets.
3. Sift the flour and salt into a
mixing bowl.
4. Stir in the sugar.
5. Cut the margarine into small
pieces then rub into flour. Knead
lightly until you have a smooth
dough.
6. Divde the dough into two equal
parts.
7. Knead a few drops of vanilla
essence into half of the dough.
8. Knead the cocoa into the other
half of the dough, making sure it
is well blended.
9. Divide each piece of dough into
half. Form each piece into an
20cm (8 inch) roll.
10. Place a vanilla roll next to a
chocolate roll, so they are side by
side. Place a vanilla roll on top of
the chocolate roll. Place the
remaining chocolate roll on top of
the vanilla roll.
11. Press all the dough lightly
together so it is joined.
12. Cut the roll into 26 slices and
put on prepared baking sheets.
13. Bake in centre of preheated
oven for 25–30 minutes, or until
firm. Leave to cool. Store in an
airtight tin and eat within 10
days.

=== COOK'S TIP ===

When mixed, this biscuit dough is
short and crumbly, so knead well as
it does not have a liquid to bind it,
just like a true shortbread.

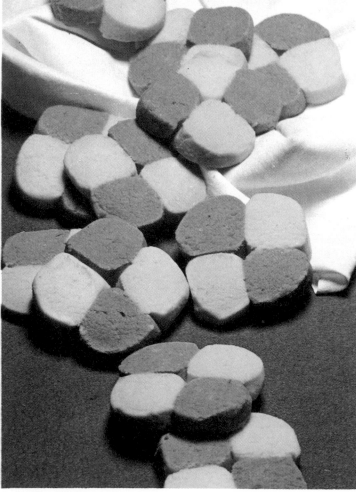

△ *Chocolate oat biscuits are crunchy
bars dipped in milk or plain
chocolate.*

◁ *Chocolate fancies are made from
half vanilla and half chocolate
biscuit dough. Keep for special
occasions.*

Index